Damola,
God's...
[signature]

PIERCING
the
spirit of the Sadducees

Akin Akinyemi
with akin Olunloyo

authorHOUSE®

AuthorHouse™ UK Ltd.
500 Avebury Boulevard
Central Milton Keynes, MK9 2BE
www.authorhouse.co.uk
Phone: 08001974150

First published by AuthorHouse 7/8/2009
© 2009 Akin Akinyemi. All rights reserved.

Published in association with

SYNCTERFACE

Syncterface Media
London
www.syncterface.com/syncterfacemedia/sots

Cover Design Concept: Syncterface Media

This book is printed on acid-free paper.

Foreword

These are very challenging times for the church. In Matthew 5:13 – 16 Jesus gives us an insight into the purpose of the church using two symbols that could be easily understood – salt and light. What was common to both was their inherent ability to bring about change. A simple yet graphic picture of the church.

The church of our Lord and Saviour Jesus Christ is the greatest reformatory vehicle that has ever been created. Its purpose is to transform lives, communities and nations. When it is unable to perform this function it is 'good for nothing but to be cast out and trodden under the foot of men'. It is derided, despised, ignored and perceived as irrelevant.

I have known Akin Akinyemi and Akin Olunloyo for quite a long time. This book, whilst born out of personal spiritual experiences speaks clearly to the church at a time when it would seem to 'have lost his savour'. Bold and obviously written from hearts that are burdened with seeing a church that has lost so much of its glory, this book is not afraid to gore anybody's ox. Whether you agree with the authors or not about what name to call the spirit, you can hardly disagree with their revelation and insight into the schemes, deceits and plans of the kingdom of darkness and its efforts to destroy the human race. The thief does come 'to steal, to kill and destroy'. I hope this book will be read by many, but I particularly hope it will be read by as many ministers of the gospel as can get hold of a copy.

It is certainly an arrow released from the kingdom of God against the kingdom of darkness. May it hit its target. Amen.

Agu Irukwu
Senior Pastor, Jesus House , London.

Comments

I always knew that there were new prophetic voices that God was going to release in the end times that will bring new layers of revelation to the body of Christ and shed new light on old truths. What I did not know was that one of those voices would come from the same womb from which I came! My very own brother.

I have not come across any book that is able to cover the issues of identity in Christ, faith in God, Christian character and the work of the Holy Spirit, as well as capture with such depth and insight, the prophetic calendar of God – all in one volume. Talk of a manual for the believer, the leader, the layperson, the minister, ...this is it.

Dr Wale Akinyemi
Founder, International Faith Embassies, Kenya.

If you are looking for a book that is inspired by the Holy Spirit and applicable to all races, culture, ethnicity and creed, this is the book. Jesus once asked His disciples "But who do you say that I am" and in reply Peter said "You are the Christ." Mark 8:27-30. This book mirrors this statement in that it dispels obscurity whilst laying greater emphasis on the need for a revelation of the person of Jesus Christ as Peter acknowledged.

In my opinion, the motto of this book is "speed with essence." I truly recommend this book to everyone seeking a fresh revelation from God. This is the key to daily Christian living.

Dr Julius Babayemi
Omnipark Dental Surgery, Kent, United Kingdom.

Appreciation

Bukola, my wife, for believing in me when all else failed and for your outstanding contribution towards completing the manuscript.

Neil, my son and Teniola, my princess who though my children, gave me counsel beyond their years and gave up many hours with them so I could complete this work.

Akin and Debisi Olunloyo, great helpers in word and deed, that stick closer than a brother.

To Korede Olunloyo, for your outstanding contribution towards completing the manuscript.

To my brother's Akinyinka and Akinwale, for their financial contribution to this assignment.

To Pastor E. A. Adeboye, for the BLESSING and unlocking the destiny of a generation.

To Bishop David Oyedepo, for unlocking the gift of God in me through his obedience to the voice of God. It was through you, that this grace came upon my life.

To Pastor Agu Irukwu, Thank you. For being a shepherd and a father, taking time to review the manuscript and writing the foreword.

To Pastor Ghandi Olaoye, Thank you. Your financial contribution has opened a new chapter.

To the exceptional teachers at Jesus House Academy, for the prayer support, the time spent reading the manuscript and for the encouraging words to ensure this work was completed.

Contents

Preface

*O*n the pages you are about to read are the thoughts that began to flood my mind after months of pain and tears; crying to the Lord in the middle of the night; pacing the paths of Dartford Central Park, believing and trusting Jesus that I will reach that moment when time and destiny will coincide to reveal purpose.

I longed for that moment when the light of heaven would shine on the contradiction of faith that faced me; where my understanding and thoughts would be exchanged with the thoughts and mind of Christ. I had stepped out in faith and everything went contrary to my expectation until suddenly...

...the light started to shine and I discovered that Jesus does not respond to my needs. He is simply attracted by my faith. The presence of fear in me clearly indicated that faith was absent, or at least not enough for the issues at hand.

This book represents the interpretation Jesus by the Holy Spirit, gave me concerning a vision I had seen. When I awoke from the experience, I quickly got a piece of paper and started to write. A number of days later, He spoke to me and said, **"There is a window of opportunity; with the same speed at which you would have written a business proposal, write this vision in a book."**

Over the next three days I wrote a significant portion of the contents of this book, majority of which I did not know before I started writing. The words flowed like water from an open tap as I wrote both day and night.

As I wrote, I compared with scriptures and found the thoughts to be accurate. I then subjected it to those God had placed over me and with me, especially akin Olunloyo, to confirm that it was not an emotionally charged expedition but a true spiritual experience.

The contribution of akin Olunloyo to this work is invaluable. He spent countless hours questioning my thoughts and validating the soundness of doctrine ensuring that I wrote down what I meant. Without his effort, vital details would have been left out.

Even though prior to this I had spent days studying the Word of God, fasting and praying, mainly in the Spirit, I believe this experience has more to do with the timing of heaven coinciding with the actions of a man desiring the depths of God.

I pray these same thoughts will liberate you and cause you to discover depths of faith that will transform your life and prepare you for the coming of the Lord, Our Master. Amen.

1

The Visions

I want to share with you two spiritual experiences that happened about twenty years apart. I discuss these with all humility knowing that it is only by His grace and election that I am still in the faith.

> [15]*But when it pleased God, who separated me from my mother's womb, and called me by his grace,*
>
> [16]*To reveal his Son in me, that I might preach him among the heathen; immediately I conferred not with flesh and blood:*

Galatians 1:15-16

I believe the time and the hour is now!

My Hour of Entry

I was born in the month of February in Scotland. My mother, who is now with Jesus, told me that my expected delivery date was meant to be a little later, but she had realised that the baby in her womb (*me*) was becoming less active so she decided to see the doctor.

On examination, the doctor discovered I had stopped taking nutrients from my mother and considering that the delivery date was near, he would recommend that she be induced. During the delivery, I came out in such a hurry that the medical team were not prepared for my speedy exit from the womb. In the rush to catch me, a member of the team tipped a bottle of iodine which splashed on my head. The burn was immediate and the scar remains till this very day.

This minor incident revealed a much bigger challenge: *I did not cry!* The doctor found that unusual and took me in for an examination. According to their results, my larynx, also known as the voicebox, was not properly formed and it was likely that I would not be able to talk. Well, thank Jesus for Godly mothers. She turned to the Lord in prayer saying she asked for a complete child and that is the outcome she expects. Now, people complain that my voice is too loud and that I talk too much. I simply say, it was my mother's fault.

As I saw Jesus the Christ, I knew it was Him. This experience happened in a moment of time.

This experience, and the visions I am about to share with you, make me understand why the enemy wanted me from the womb.

The Vision - 19th November 1989

I had just given my life to the Lord and I was spending some time with my grandmother, along with my brother, his friends, our cousins and a few others. My grandfather was a Bishop in the Anglican Community and he had a chapel in his house where prayers at 6:00am and 8:00pm were an everyday constant. As long as you lived under his roof, attending these prayer sessions was not an option.

On the 19th of November 1989, in a prayer meeting, that was led by my brother, I had a vision. As Paul said, whether in the body or out of the body, I cannot tell. Shortly before this experience, I remember my brother saying, "Some of you here are going to have supernatural experiences". Then suddenly, I found myself walking with a man down what seemed like a street; the clouds held us up as we walked. I did not need anyone to tell me who He was. As I saw Jesus the Christ, I knew it was Him. As we walked, He was giving me specific instructions regarding an assignment.

After a while, Jesus told me to kneel down. He put something in my hands and said to me, "**Go and give them**". I was not sure what it was or who I was meant to give it to. As I was about to ask, Jesus answered instantaneously as if He was reading my mind, "**I will reveal it to you**

when the time is come." This is the first time I am putting this vision in writing. I have only mentioned it to a limited number of people and the reason I mention it now is because of another experience I had on the 31st of December 2008.

The Vision - 31st December 2008.

Some months after Jesus had asked me to take some time off what I was doing and prepare for a land He was going to show me, I started to pray fervently. Not that I was not a prayerful person before, but prayer just took on a whole new meaning as circumstances and events of my life had presented me with no other option. I was at a point where my thoughts were about to be exchanged for His thoughts and my ways for His ways.

My "*tried and tested*" methods had failed to deliver the much needed results and I quickly realised something was missing. In order to fill this void, I spent long hours seeking God; following the anointed teaching of trusted men of God, personally studying the scriptures and praying in the Spirit endlessly. I engaged in extended sessions of worship into the late hours of the night asking God to show me what was missing using Paul the apostle's prayer for the church in Ephesus:

[15]*Wherefore I also, after I heard of your faith in the Lord Jesus, and love unto all the saints,*

[16]*Cease not to give thanks for you, making mention of you in my prayers;*

[17]*That the God of our Lord Jesus Christ, the Father of glory, may give unto you the spirit of wisdom and revelation in the knowledge of him:*

[18]*The eyes of your understanding being enlightened; that ye may know what is the hope of his calling, and what the riches of the glory of his inheritance in the saints,*

[19]*And what is the exceeding greatness of his power to us-ward who believe, according to the working of his mighty power,*

[20]*Which he wrought in Christ, when he raised him from the dead, and set him at his own right hand in the heavenly places,*

[21]*Far above all principality, and power, and might, and dominion, and every name that is named, not only in this world, but also in that which is to come:*

[22]*And hath put all things under his feet, and gave him to be the head over all things to the church,*

[23]Which is his body, the fulness of him that filleth all in all

Ephesians 1:15-23

I had asked Jesus to use dreams, visions, the inward witness and whatever means possible to let me know what was missing as I had become troubled in my spirit. Then suddenly, I started having all manner of dreams which seemed to convey certain information. Some were related while others were completely disjointed, but I always checked for accuracy with the scriptures. Then came December the 31st.

I went to bed in the early hours of the morning of the 31st and suddenly I found myself at the north end of what looked like an enclosed swimming pool area. In a corner of the pool there was what I can only call a feeding stand. I noticed someone throwing what looked like very large chunks of meat into the water as though the person was feeding some sort of animal. It was similar to the way I had seen crocodiles being fed. I then noticed a creature that looked and walked like a crocodile. It was crawling on the northern side of the pool and it descended into the water.

Then I found myself at the south end of the pool, between two large doors. One of the doors opened into the pool area and the other opened into the real world. Now, nobody told me it was the real world, I just knew. The door that led to the pool area had two small holes in the middle and I heard the sound of worship coming out of the area. A voice said to me, "**Look through the hole**".

Instantly, lightning appeared from the heavens and struck the beast.

When I looked through the hole, I noticed a few things. On the other side of the door there was a bigger crocodile compared to the one I had seen earlier. This time, the creature was walking towards the north-east corner of the pool from the southern side. From the north-east corner came the sound of songs that sounded like worship from a church service. Many people were going in and out as though they were working in shifts. I recognised the faces of some worship leaders and I believe this is why I associated the sound from that corner with church worship.

While I was looking through the hole, someone came out of the pool area into where I was, between the two doors. The voice guiding me said, "***That is the speaker***". I instantly knew that the speaker represented people and ministers that were getting results but these results were not given by Jesus. ***They were false signs.***

At the south-west corner of the pool was another sound of worship. This sounded purer than the sound coming from the north-east corner. The voice that was guiding me said, "***Those are the remnants***". Instantly, the story of Elijah the prophet came to mind; when Elijah thought he was the only one remaining that served God and the Lord told him that there were seven thousand other prophets that had not bowed their knee to baal.

> [10]*And he said, I have been very jealous for the LORD God of hosts: for the children of Israel have forsaken thy covenant, thrown down thine altars, and slain thy prophets with the sword; and I, even I only, am left; and they seek my life, to take it away.*
>
> [11]*And he said, Go forth, and stand upon the mount before the LORD. And, behold, the LORD passed by, and a great and strong wind rent the mountains, and brake in pieces the rocks before the LORD; but the LORD was not in the wind: and after the wind an earthquake; but the LORD was not in the earthquake:*
>
> [12]*And after the earthquake a fire; but the LORD was not in the fire: and after the fire a still small voice.*
>
> [13]*And it was so, when Elijah heard it, that he wrapped his face in his mantle, and went out, and stood in the entering in of the cave. And, behold, there came a voice unto him, and said, What doest thou here, Elijah?*
>
> [14]*And he said, I have been very jealous for the LORD God of hosts: because the children of Israel have forsaken thy covenant, thrown down thine altars, and slain thy prophets with the sword; and I, even I only, am left; and they seek my life, to take it away.*
>
> [15]*And the LORD said unto him, Go, return on thy way to the wilderness of Damascus: and when thou comest, anoint Hazael to be king over Syria:*
>
> [16]*And Jehu the son of Nimshi shalt thou anoint to be king over Israel: and Elisha the son of Shaphat of Abelmeholah shalt thou anoint to be prophet in thy room.*
>
> [17]*And it shall come to pass, that him that escapeth the sword of Hazael shall Jehu slay: and him that escapeth from the sword of Jehu shall Elisha slay.*

> [18]*Yet I have left me seven thousand in Israel, all the knees which have not bowed unto Baal, and every mouth which hath not kissed him.*
>
> **1 Kings 19:10-18**

Suddenly, a creature began to rise from the centre of the pool. It looked like an old Egyptian sphinx. In a flash, the skin on its face changed to what looked like the skin that was on the crocodile-like creature and it turned into a fierce looking beast.

Instantly, lightning appeared from the heavens and struck the beast. In a moment of time, as I watched, Jesus brought back the vision from the 19th November 1989 and showed me how He had prepared me for now. I remember being amazed at how accurate the events of the past had been in ensuring that, before the beast arose from the waters, God had already raised His army.

As I stood between the doors and watched the events unfolding, I realised I was not alone. The voice guiding me told me that I was not alone; that there were many people who had been prepared and were seeing the same thing. As these events unfolded I began to tremble. When I *awoke* from this experience, my physical body was shaking. Instinctively, I looked for a piece of paper to draw what I had seen and the specific words that came to me. The dreams, some of which gave further clarification of the vision, continued for about a week then stopped.

As the days went by, I wondered in my heart what these visions and dreams meant and I asked the Lord to explain them to me. As I meditated on these things, I decided to spend time away from my normal environment and went to a park close to where I live. I walked around the park and prayed in the Spirit, ignoring the many faces that turned to look at me and wondered what I was saying. I did this for about three days. On the third day, the heavens opened as I suddenly started to pray like someone in labour, and did not stop until I knew I had taken delivery of the message and I heard an instruction from God telling me to write the vision in a book.

Later that day, while driving, the Holy Spirit spoke to me and said, "***the***

spirit of the Sadducees". Flashing through my mind was the image of a dark cloud descending on the Church and only *truth* as revealed by the Holy Spirit and uttered by believers could pierce a hole in the cloud.

Immediately, I knew that the beast arising from within the pool represented *the spirit of the Sadducees* that wants to bring darkness on the church through deception. This was characterised by the changing face of the beast in the vision and the worshippers who seemed to be worshipping the true God.

Now, by His grace, I will shed more light on what God dropped in my heart about *the spirit of the Sadducees.* This book is the cry of an unlearned one regarding a change in spiritual order and with it, I begin to deliver the message the Lord has committed into my hands.

2

Who were the Pharisees and the Sadducees?

*T*he Pharisees and Sadducees were both Jewish sects. From the Gospels, the constant conflict and deceptive questions they presented to Jesus could not go unnoticed.

¹The Pharisees also with the Sadducees came, and tempting desired him that he would shew them a sign from heaven.

²He answered and said unto them, When it is evening, ye say, It will be fair weather: for the sky is red.

³And in the morning, It will be foul weather to day: for the sky is red and lowering. O ye hypocrites, ye can discern the face of the sky; but can ye not discern the signs of the times?

Matthew 16:1-3

While the Scriptures more often than not referred to these two sects together, they were distinctively different.

The Sadducees on the other hand were the religious rationalists, the aristocrats and holders of powerful positions.

The Pharisees were mostly middle-class businessmen. Though they were a minority in the Jewish Ruling council i.e. the Sanhedrin, they seemed to control the decision making of the Council because they had the support of the common man. The Pharisees religiously accepted the written Word as inspired by God but insisted that traditions had equal authority. They did however remain true to God's word with reference to certain important doctrines:

- The Pharisees believed that God has foreknowledge of human destiny
- The Pharisees believed in the resurrection of the dead

⁶But when Paul perceived that the one part were Sadducees, and the other Pharisees, he cried out in the council, Men and brethren, I am a Pharisee, the son of a Pharisee: of the hope and resurrection of the dead I am called in question.

Acts 23:6

- The Pharisees believed in the afterlife
- They believed in the existence of angels and demons

  ⁸For the Sadducees say that there is no resurrection, neither angel, nor spirit: but the Pharisees confess both.

  Acts 23:8

The Sadducees on the other hand were the religious rationalists, the aristocrats and holders of powerful positions. They were the chief priests and controlled the majority in the Sanhedrin. The Sadducees held the written Word of God, particularly those written by Moses, in very high regard. As a result, they held significant political clout which was used as means of institutionalising religious practices of the Law of Moses. Apostle Paul later referred to this written Word of God as "the Letter".

⁶Who also hath made us able ministers of the new testament; not of the letter, but of the spirit: FOR THE LETTER KILLETH, but the spirit giveth life.

2 Corinthians 3:6

Here are some of their beliefs that contradict Scripture:

- They were extremely self sufficient to the point of denying God's involvement in everyday life.
- They denied any resurrection of the dead

  ²³The same day came to him the Sadducees, which say that there is no resurrection, and asked him,

  Matthew 22:23

- They denied any afterlife, holding that the soul perished at death
- They denied the existence of a spiritual world, i.e. angels and demons

These were the main differences in the beliefs of these two sects.

Matthew 23 says a lot more about the Pharisees. However, as the word of the Lord that came to me specifically referred to the *spirit of the Sadducees*, I will now focus solely on the *Sadducees*.

As you open your heart and read the following chapters of this book, I believe you will receive insight of eternal value.

3

The spirit of the Sadducees

The spirit of the Sadducees is a deceptive, selfish, ruling spirit with the ability to transform itself like an angel of light. This appearance of light makes it possible for it to find its way into vantage positions in organisations, including the Church. It is the spirit in operation in false christs.

The spirit of the Sadducees is the spirit behind distorted and compromised words that are presented as the mind of God. It is the spirit that elevates the letter of the word of God above spiritual insight and Godly wisdom. This spirit seeks to seduce the chosen in Christ through the use of lying signs and wonders.

Jesus and Apostle Paul spoke about this spirit and warned the elect not to be deceived.

> *[22]For false Christs and false prophets shall rise, and shall shew signs and wonders, to seduce, if it were possible, even the elect.*
>
> *[23]But take ye heed: behold, I have foretold you all things.*

Mark 13:22-23

> *[13]For such are false apostles, deceitful workers, transforming themselves into the apostles of Christ.*
>
> *[14]And no marvel; for Satan himself is transformed into an angel of light.*

2 Corinthians 11:13-14

God is speaking to believers again today, warning that this deceptive spirit is rising from the place of darkness and the church needs to be aware of its signs. This spirit was at work in the Sadducees in the time of Jesus, denying the existence of the spiritual. It replaced spirituality with traditions, shielding people from the effect of the Word of God.

Our understanding of the operation of these ruling spirits is important because they can only be overcome by spiritual revelation and wisdom from the word of God. The Sadducees always came to Jesus with trick questions and situations, hoping to trap him thereby ensnaring Him with His own words and on every occasion Jesus responded with spiritual insight.

> *[23]And when he was come into the temple, the chief priests and the elders of the people came unto him as he was teaching, and said, By what authority doest thou these things? and who gave thee this authority?*
>
> *[24]And Jesus answered and said unto them, I also will ask you one thing, which if ye tell me, I in like wise will tell you by what authority I do these things.*
>
> *[25]The baptism of John, whence was it? from heaven, or of men? And they reasoned with themselves, saying, If we shall say, From heaven; he will say unto us, Why did ye not then believe him?*
>
> *[26]But if we shall say, Of men; we fear the people; for all hold John as a prophet.*
>
> *[27]And they answered Jesus, and said, We cannot tell. And he said unto them, Neither tell I you by what authority I do these things.*

Matthew 21:23-27

As the grip of political correctness tightens on our world, spiritual insight is needed now more than ever before. The attempt to test the wisdom of our teaching is going to rise beyond measure. Our response in these situations is what will break the hold of this ruling spirit and put it in its place.

> *[23]The same day came to him the Sadducees, which say that there is no resurrection, and asked him,*
>
> *[24]Saying, Master, Moses said, If a man die, having no children, his brother shall marry his wife, and raise up seed unto his brother.*
>
> *[25]Now there were with us seven brethren: and the first, when he had married a wife, deceased, and, having no issue, left his wife unto his brother:*
>
> *[26]Likewise the second also, and the third, unto the seventh.*
>
> *[27]And last of all the woman died also.*
>
> *[28]Therefore in the resurrection whose wife shall she be of the seven? for they all had her.*
>
> *[29]Jesus answered and said unto them, Ye do err, not knowing the scriptures, nor the power of God.*

[30]For in the resurrection they neither marry, nor are given in marriage, but are as the angels of God in heaven.

[31]But as touching the resurrection of the dead, have ye not read that which was spoken unto you by God, saying,

[32]I am the God of Abraham, and the God of Isaac, and the God of Jacob? God is not the God of the dead, but of the living.

[33]And when the multitude heard this, they were astonished at his doctrine.

Matthew 22:23-33

The words of the Sadducees were always theoretical and idealistic and it takes the Holy Spirit to provide the believer with spiritual insight beyond the reasoning of these Sadducees. (*Luke 21:15*)

The spirit of the Sadducees is a deceptive, ruling spirit with the ability to transform itself like an angel of light.

The term "Sadducees" was referred to only nine times in the Gospels. The first was in *Matthew 3* when John the Baptist identified their lineage, representing the involvement of this spirit in affairs of the family. The next four were in *Matthew 16*, where Jesus warned about their doctrine, and the last four gave the account of how Jesus silenced them. {*There are other accounts of the Sadducees in scripture referring to them as chief priests, describing the role they performed in society and organised religion*}.

The context in *Matthew 16* makes the doctrine Jesus spoke about very relevant to the days we are in. Following the warning on the doctrine of the Sadducees to the disciples, came the revelation of the true Christ and the first mention of the Church or called out ones having access to the keys of heaven to exercise dominion and authority in the earth. Jesus continues in this same encounter to talk to His disciples about His second coming.

[12]Then understood they how that he bade them not beware of the leaven of bread, but of the doctrine of the Pharisees and of the Sadducees.

[13]When Jesus came into the coasts of Caesarea Philippi, he asked his disciples, saying, Whom do men say that I the Son of man am?

^{14}And they said, Some say that thou art John the Baptist: some, Elias; and others, Jeremias, or one of the prophets.

^{15}He saith unto them, But whom say ye that I am?

^{16}And Simon Peter answered and said, Thou art the Christ, the Son of the living God.

^{17}And Jesus answered and said unto him, Blessed art thou, Simon Barjona: for flesh and blood hath not revealed it unto thee, but my Father which is in heaven.

^{18}And I say also unto thee, That thou art Peter, and upon this rock I will build my church; and the gates of hell shall not prevail against it.

^{19}And I will give unto thee the keys of the kingdom of heaven: and whatsoever thou shalt bind on earth shall be bound in heaven: and whatsoever thou shalt loose on earth shall be loosed in heaven.

Matthew 16:12-19

^{27}For the Son of man shall come in the glory of his Father with his angels; and then he shall reward every man according to his works.

Matthew 16:27

Jesus is coming back for His glorified Church, His bride. He is again warning the Church about these doctrines and His second coming.

4

The spirit of the Sadducees is Deceptive

This spirit is a deceptive spirit. It attempts to blind minds to the truth of the word of God. It presents alternative actions to the instructions of the Holy Spirit making things seem right to believers but those that are grounded in the word of God will not be deceived. The Lord Himself will provide interpretation of scripture.

The Holy Spirit, with the help of a concordance, helped me expand the words "**serpent**", to mean the enchanter that casts a spell in a whisper or hiss and "**subtil**", to mean to come up with crafty counsel to produce undesirable or ungodly results. When these definitions are inserted in *Genesis 3* it reads:

> *¹Now the serpent (the enchanter that casts a spell in a whisper or hiss) was more subtil (had more ability to come up with crafty counsel to produce undesirable or ungodly results) than any beast of the field which the LORD God had made. And he said unto the woman, Yea, hath God said, Ye shall not eat of every tree of the garden?*
>
> *²And the woman said unto the serpent, We may eat of the fruit of the trees of the garden:*
>
> *³But of the fruit of the tree which is in the midst of the garden, God hath said, Ye shall not eat of it, neither shall ye touch it, lest ye die.*
>
> *⁴And the serpent said unto the woman, Ye shall not surely die:*
>
> *⁵For God doth know that in the day ye eat thereof, then your eyes shall be opened, and ye shall be as gods, knowing good and evil.*
>
> *⁶And when the woman saw that the tree was good for food, and that it was pleasant to the eyes, and a tree to be desired to make one wise, she took of the fruit thereof, and did eat, and gave also unto her husband with her; and he did eat.*

Genesis 3:1-6

Its operation as recorded in the deception of Adam and Eve shows a spirit of earthly wisdom that makes a thing seem right to a man but the end therefore is death. It seeks to take the word of God and bring out contrary *spiritual* wisdom or interpretation. It even attempts to speak authoritatively against the word of God.

> *4And the serpent said unto the woman, Ye shall not surely die:*

> **Genesis 3:4**

It was through deception that the devil was able to get Eve to eat the fruit. He presented the fruit as what it was not.

> *13And the LORD God said unto the woman, What is this that thou hast done? And the woman said, The serpent beguiled me, and I did eat.*

> **Genesis 3:13**

We always wonder how Eve was tempted and eventually deceived. Apostle James puts it like this:

> *14But every man is tempted, when he is drawn away of his own lust, and enticed.*
> *15Then when lust hath conceived, it bringeth forth sin: and sin, when it is finished, bringeth forth death.*

> **James 1:14-15**

If Eve entertained thoughts that considered what eating the fruit of the tree of the knowledge of good and evil was like, this was enough for the enchanter to cast his spell (*Matthew 5:28*). It is exactly the same today, the devil is constantly seeking whom he may destroy and many believers are taking his bait even though we know that continually staying in the place of temptation without the Word of God weakens our resistance.

---

though a tangible need exists, the labour for the prophetic word should have pre-eminence over the physical labour or activities required to meet the need.

The bible warns us to abstain from all appearances of evil. In another place, we are warned to flee lusts. Comparing this account with the temptation of Jesus, we notice three different forms of deception.

> *1And Jesus being full of the Holy Ghost returned from Jordan, and was led by the Spirit into the wilderness,*

[2] Being forty days tempted of the devil. And in those days he did eat nothing: and when they were ended, he afterward hungered.

[3] And the devil said unto him, If thou be the Son of God, command this stone that it be made bread.

[4] And Jesus answered him, saying, It is written, That man shall not live by bread alone, but by every word of God.

[5] And the devil, taking him up into an high mountain, shewed unto him all the kingdoms of the world in a moment of time.

[6] And the devil said unto him, All this power will I give thee, and the glory of them: for that is delivered unto me; and to whomsoever I will I give it.

[7] If thou therefore wilt worship me, all shall be thine.

[8] And Jesus answered and said unto him, Get thee behind me, Satan: for it is written, Thou shalt worship the Lord thy God, and him only shalt thou serve.

[9] And he brought him to Jerusalem, and set him on a pinnacle of the temple, and said unto him, If thou be the Son of God, cast thyself down from hence:

[10] For it is written, He shall give his angels charge over thee, to keep thee:

[11] And in their hands they shall bear thee up, lest at any time thou dash thy foot against a stone.

[12] And Jesus answering said unto him, It is said, Thou shalt not tempt the Lord thy God.

[13] And when the devil had ended all the temptation, he departed from him for a season.

[14] And Jesus returned in the power of the Spirit into Galilee: and there went out a fame of him through all the region round about.

Luke 4:1-14

Deception of Needs

This form of deception is based on individual needs. *Deuteronomy 8:3* indicates that the reason God provided manna in the wilderness for the children of Israel was not just to feed them but God was proving to them that their material requirements for sustenance in this earth could be provided by the fulfilment of prophetic declarations. These prophetic declarations refer to the inspired words that come out of our spirit man and the words we receive through the ministry of anointed men and women of God.

[3] And he humbled thee, and suffered thee to hunger, and fed thee with manna, which thou knewest not, neither did thy fathers know; that he might make thee know that man doth not live by bread only, but by every word that proceedeth out of the mouth of the LORD doth man live.

[4]Thy raiment waxed not old upon thee, neither did thy foot swell, these forty years.

Deuteronomy 8:3-4

As a result of the prophetic word that proceeded from God, the bible declares that though they lived and walked in the wilderness for forty years,their clothes did not grow old and their feet did not swell.

The temptation of Jesus to turn stones to bread was the devil trying to get Jesus to use His indwelling ability to meet his hunger for material things without the prophetic declaration of the word of God. Jesus responded by saying that though a tangible need exists, the labour for the prophetic word should have pre-eminence over the physical labour or activities required to meet the need.

It is the deception that make believers think they cannot change governments, laws or policies without holding authoritative positions in the kingdoms of the world.

Apostle Paul explained this to the Corinthian Church when he described the necessary ingredients for fruitfulness.

[6]I have planted, Apollos watered; but God gave the increase.

[7]So then neither is he that planteth any thing, neither he that watereth; but God that giveth the increase.

1 Corinthians 3:6-7

A fruitful experience for the believer requires planting, watering and increase. The *increase* here is released through prophetic declarations and is something God provides. ***Everything we engage in as believers should have a corresponding spiritual instruction.*** It is the presence of this instruction that eliminates toil in the work of our hands. Toil is the description of activities that have no spiritual instruction behind them. This is when productivity is less than activity.

Deception of Authority

This is the form of deception where the believer thinks they need to occupy a position of authority before the works of the kingdom can be done. It is the deception that make believers think they cannot change governments, laws or policies without holding authoritative positions in the kingdoms of the world. The kingdom of the world and the kingdom of our God are separate and the two do not mix.

The real things of God that can make a difference in society have no law against them. There is no law against loving our neighbours. There is no law that forbids us from giving to eradicate poverty. More importantly, the position in the kingdom of God and the authority we need to be able to do these things have been given to us. Our commitment to the service of our God will overturn any earthly law that restricts us.

In the book of Daniel, we see the story of three Hebrew boys who changed the words of a king. Their position in the government of the time did not place them high enough to even have their opinions sought before laws were passed, yet by their actions, they influenced society for good.

> [1]*Nebuchadnezzar the king made an image of gold, whose height was threescore cubits, and the breadth thereof six cubits: he set it up in the plain of Dura, in the province of Babylon.*
>
> [2]*Then Nebuchadnezzar the king sent to gather together the princes, the governors, and the captains, the judges, the treasurers, the counsellors, the sheriffs, and all the rulers of the provinces, to come to the dedication of the image which Nebuchadnezzar the king had set up.*
>
> [3]*Then the princes, the governors, and captains, the judges, the treasurers, the counsellors, the sheriffs, and all the rulers of the provinces, were gathered together unto the dedication of the image that Nebuchadnezzar the king had set up; and they stood before the image that Nebuchadnezzar had set up.*
>
> [4]*Then an herald cried aloud, To you it is commanded, O people, nations, and languages,*
>
> [5]*That at what time ye hear the sound of the cornet, flute, harp, sackbut, psaltery, dulcimer, and all kinds of musick, ye fall down and worship the golden image that Nebuchadnezzar the king hath set up:*
>
> [6]*And whoso falleth not down and worshippeth shall the same hour be cast into the midst of a burning fiery furnace.*

[7]Therefore at that time, when all the people heard the sound of the cornet, flute, harp, sackbut, psaltery, and all kinds of musick, all the people, the nations, and the languages, fell down and worshipped the golden image that Nebuchadnezzar the king had set up.

[8]Wherefore at that time certain Chaldeans came near, and accused the Jews.

[9]They spake and said to the king Nebuchadnezzar, O king, live for ever.

[10]Thou, O king, hast made a decree, that every man that shall hear the sound of the cornet, flute, harp, sackbut, psaltery, and dulcimer, and all kinds of musick, shall fall down and worship the golden image:

[11]And whoso falleth not down and worshippeth, that he should be cast into the midst of a burning fiery furnace.

[12]There are certain Jews whom thou hast set over the affairs of the province of Babylon, Shadrach, Meshach, and Abednego; these men, O king, have not regarded thee: they serve not thy gods, nor worship the golden image which thou hast set up.

[13]Then Nebuchadnezzar in his rage and fury commanded to bring Shadrach, Meshach, and Abednego. Then they brought these men before the king.

Daniel 3:1-13

Our commitment to the service of our God will overturn any earthly law that restricts us.

---

[27]And the princes, governors, and captains, and the king's counsellors, being gathered together, saw these men, upon whose bodies the fire had no power, nor was an hair of their head singed, neither were their coats changed, nor the smell of fire had passed on them.

[28]Then Nebuchadnezzar spake, and said, Blessed be the God of Shadrach, Meshach, and Abednego, who hath sent his angel, and delivered his servants that trusted in him, and have changed the king's word, and yielded their bodies, that they might not serve nor worship any god, except their own God.

[29]Therefore I make a decree, That every people, nation, and language, which speak any thing amiss against the God of Shadrach, Meshach, and Abednego, shall be cut in pieces, and their houses shall be made a dunghill: because there is no other God that can deliver after this sort.

[30]Then the king promoted Shadrach, Meshach, and Abednego, in the province of Babylon.

Daniel 3:27-30

If believers do not stand strong in trusting and serving the Lord, the people of the land suffer and the relevance of the relationship we have with our God is questioned. Our authority is not from this earth, our authority is from above and this authority cannot be challenged.

Deception of the word

This form of deception attempts to trigger actions from the believer that are based on the misinterpreted word of God. The third temptation of Jesus is the only one of the temptations according to Luke that happened at the pinnacle of the temple in Jerusalem, the city of God. In modern times, this temptation is the temptation that takes place in the Church.

The location of this temptation is significant. Most people tend to drop their guard in the presence of those they trust. Adam dropped his guard with Eve and paid dearly for it. The temptation of Adam that separated him from God was not one that took place outside the Garden of Eden. It took place within the garden of the Lord.

One of the greatest challenges this new dispensation of God will overcome is not coming from outside the Church. It is the battle to overcome doctrines that have no basis in the word of God, being preached in the Church. These are doctrines that have emanated as a result of the experiences of the peddlers and not ones that have come through revelation from the word of God. These are words that sound right but cannot be validated by the word of God.

For example, we justify prolonged sickness in the body because the Lord may be trying to teach us something or He may be trying to humble us. We even state that when Apostle Paul had a problem and went to God concerning this issue, the Lord pointed him to grace.

> *[7]And lest I should be exalted above measure through the abundance of the revelations, there was given to me a thorn in the flesh, the messenger of Satan to buffet me, lest I should be exalted above measure.*
>
> *[8]For this thing I besought the Lord thrice, that it might depart from me.*
>
> *[9]And he said unto me, My grace is sufficient for thee: for my strength is made perfect in weakness. Most gladly therefore will I rather glory in my infirmities, that the power of Christ may rest upon me.*

> [10]*Therefore I take pleasure in infirmities, in reproaches, in necessities, in persecutions, in distresses for Christ's sake: for when I am weak, then am I strong.*
>
> **2 Corinthians 12:7-10**

However, looking at Jesus the author and finisher of our faith, there is no record in scripture of Jesus needing healing. Divine health is the plan of God. Healing is His provision for us when we fall short of divine health. There is no record of Jesus having a need that was not met and Jesus is the image of God that we need to aspire to. People who experience God through divine healing will always describe God as a healer but He is more than a healer. He is our strength and our health.

There is no negative or evil challenge we face whose source is God.

We accept that challenges do occur and when they do, we overcome. There is no negative or evil challenge we face that has its source in God. However, God is able to make these challenges to work in our favour. We must remember that there is no challenge we face or will ever face that should be significant enough to make us take our focus off God.

5

The spirit of the Sadducees seeks to Rule

*W*hen we hear the term *RULER*, the mind naturally goes to those that God has allowed to be in the different tiers of governing for the effective running of society. The ruling nature of this spirit goes beyond this. The spirit of the Sadducees seeks to turn leaders into rulers. It is important to understand that LEADERSHIP and RULERSHIP are two different concepts.

We could write volumes on these two concepts but one basic truth is that LEADERSHIP does not have a *"lower being"* mentality {*leadership in Christ promotes service and respect for equality*}, while RULERSHIP requires laws and promotes justification by the law {*the "lower beings" either keep the law or face the consequences of breaking it*}.

This spirit expresses itself in ruling bodies and councils. It seeks to establish rulership in formal organisations that will bring bondage and burden to the people of God. Immediately after the miracle of provision in *John 6*, the men in the place wanted to make Jesus king. They wrongly associated miracles and power with a natural position of authority. Jesus, knowing this departed alone into a mountain.

> [15]*When Jesus therefore perceived that they would come and take him by force, to make him a king, he departed again into a mountain himself alone.*

John 6:15

Jesus did not come to be a natural king; He came to establish the kingdom of God. His participation in this earthly kingdom was not a prerequisite for the establishing of the Kingdom of God. In fact, he came to destroy the law on which the kingdom of this world was based, that is, the *law of sin and death*. He fulfilled the law then abolished it with the introduction of a new law; the law of the Spirit of Life.

When the devil tempted Jesus, he offered him a position of ownership of all the kingdoms of the world. Jesus aptly rejected this proving that he did not come to participate in that kingdom; He was here to establish his own.

> *⁵And the devil, taking him up into an high mountain, shewed unto him all the kingdoms of the world in a moment of time.*
>
> *⁶And the devil said unto him, All this power will I give thee, and the glory of them: for that is delivered unto me; and to whomsoever I will I give it.*

> Luke 4:5-6

Nowadays, believers tend to turn to the strategies adopted by the world and this is only because the order in the Church is not intact. It was never the plan of God for the children of Israel to have a king. He wanted to be their King but they rejected this because of a carnal desire to be like the nations of the world.

> *¹And it came to pass, when Samuel was old, that he made his sons judges over Israel.*
>
> *²Now the name of his firstborn was Joel; and the name of his second, Abiah: they were judges in Beersheba.*
>
> *³And his sons walked not in his ways, but turned aside after lucre, and took bribes, and perverted judgment.*
>
> *⁴Then all the elders of Israel gathered themselves together, and came to Samuel unto Ramah,*
>
> *⁵And said unto him, Behold, thou art old, and thy sons walk not in thy ways: now make us a king to judge us like all the nations.*

> 1 Samuel 8:1--5

Notice that the demand for a king to provide judgement like the other nations only came after those placed in the position of authority failed to walk in the ways of God. These leaders had turned into rulers.

1 Samuel 8 paints a graphic picture of the governments of our day. Taxes are levied on the people to fund the morally derailed ethics of those in positions of authority. Errors of judgement against the people are allowed to continue because the laws of the day do not condemn such activities.

We as believers need to come against this rule, not by participating in the reformation of these institutions but by creating parallel bodies whose success will dwarf that of existing structures. Is it a wonder that the most successful institutions of learning in many countries of the world today are the ones with their roots in the Church?

> *What difference is the church making if it goes under when worldly institutions go under and rises when they rise?*

I believe the Church needs to setup its own kingdom institutions based on godly principles and let the mysteries of the kingdom of our God work in them. Imagine a banking institution with someone like Isaac directing its affairs, leading the organisation to reap one hundred fold in the midst of a deep recession (*Genesis 26:1-14*). It goes without saying that this bank would be a shining light and will naturally attract needed resources to continue to expand.

Supernatural intelligence from the Holy Spirit will make every decision profitable. This will completely eradicate ungodly expressions of this ruling spirit. What difference is the church making if it goes under when worldly institutions go under and rises when they rise?

Formal education is not a prerequisite for this expression of ministry. The availability of formal education should be promoted as long as the thoughts shared are inspirational and not theological doctrines that lack power. The Sadducees promoted legalism and watered down the power of the Word.

[1]*Paul, an apostle of Jesus Christ by the commandment of God our Saviour, and Lord Jesus Christ, which is our hope;*

[2]*Unto Timothy, my own son in the faith: Grace, mercy, and peace, from God our Father and Jesus Christ our Lord.*

[3]*As I besought thee to abide still at Ephesus, when I went into Macedonia, that thou mightest charge some that they teach no other doctrine,*

[4]*Neither give heed to fables and endless genealogies, which minister questions, rather than godly edifying which is in faith: so do.*

⁵Now the end of the commandment is charity out of a pure heart, and of a good conscience, and of faith unfeigned:

⁶From which some having swerved have turned aside unto vain jangling;

⁷Desiring to be teachers of the law; understanding neither what they say, nor whereof they affirm.

⁸But we know that the law is good, if a man use it lawfully;

1 Timothy 1:1-8

In this end time we will witness a very strong opposition from what we know to be the organised church as members of the congregation, the *unlearned and uneducated*, start to get results that years and years of formal ministry have diluted.

Many are so consumed with ministerial traditions that the manifestation of these uneducated and unlearned ones will trigger great persecution, not from the outside but from within.

Time and time again, the doctrine of Sadducees referred to the background of Jesus, confirming that there was nothing in there that prepared him for what he was doing. It was the anointing on Him that made the difference.

¹⁸The Spirit of the Lord is upon me, because he hath anointed me to preach the gospel to the poor; he hath sent me to heal the brokenhearted, to preach deliverance to the captives, and recovering of sight to the blind, to set at liberty them that are bruised,

¹⁹To preach the acceptable year of the Lord.

²⁰And he closed the book, and he gave it again to the minister, and sat down. And the eyes of all them that were in the synagogue were fastened on him.

²¹And he began to say unto them, This day is this scripture fulfilled in your ears.

²²And all bare him witness, and wondered at the gracious words which proceeded out of his mouth. And they said, IS NOT THIS JOSEPH'S SON?

Luke 4:18-22

Many in organised ministries are not prepared for the change in order coming to the body of Christ and are so consumed with ministerial traditions that the manifestation of these *uneducated and unlearned* ones will trigger great persecution, not from the outside but from within the Church.

The strength of these ones will lie in their expansion in the face of persecution. Their depth of revelation and spiritual insight will deliver what eyes have not seen and what ears have not heard. It is only those that are truly after Christ that will be able to walk in this unusual move of the Holy Spirit.

Paul the apostle spoke about this ruling spirit in the hierarchy mentioned to the church in Ephesus

> *12For we wrestle not against flesh and blood, but against principalities, against powers, against the rulers of the darkness of this world, against spiritual wickedness in high places.*

Ephesians 6:12

This change in hierarchy signifies a change in spiritual momentum and activity. Three major areas where scripture emphasises hierarchy are Finances, Family and Warfare. These are areas in which rulership is exercised. Even though I intend to delve deeper into these areas later on in this book, it is important to know that the rise of the spirit of the Sadducees is to gain rule over these three areas. However, the Spirit of the Lord has raised the remnant to do battle. This battle will be the fiercest the modern day Christian has ever known but we thank God who has given us the victory and seated us with Christ in heavenly places.

At no time in the history of the church has it been as equipped and anointed as it is now. Those that have ears to hear will hear and act; they will have oil in their lamps and their minds will be enlightened with the Gospel. Today, our focus must be on using God's principles to solve the problems of humanity. The church is the only body on earth through which the world can see God. Jesus said, "Whosoever has seen Me has seen the Father". This statement is still very true today. For anyone to see Jesus, they should simply take look at the Church.

6

The spirit of the Sadducees is Selfish

This spirit causes people to focus on self. We must realize that selfishness is what lies at the heart of self-preservation. It makes people consider the restoration of self above the restoration of the church. In the restored church, every individual need is met.

The children of Israel, though a multitude in the wilderness, did not have one feeble person among them. This state of glory was because of a covenant God had made with Abraham, Isaac and Jacob.

^{37}He brought them forth also with silver and gold: and there was not one feeble person among their tribes.

^{38}Egypt was glad when they departed: for the fear of them fell upon them.

^{39}He spread a cloud for a covering; and fire to give light in the night.

^{40}The people asked, and he brought quails, and satisfied them with the bread of heaven.

^{41}He opened the rock, and the waters gushed out; they ran in the dry places like a river.

^{42}For he remembered his holy promise, and Abraham his servant.

Psalms 105:37-42

Whenever this evil spirit enters a place there is a strong desire for self preservation. When Adam and Eve realised they were naked, their first instinct was to cover themselves. They had to go through the trouble of making themselves aprons, acquiring material things through the toil of their hands.

The evidence that we are walking in faith is our ability to use it productively on demand

---

> *7And the eyes of them both were opened, and they knew that they were naked; and they sewed fig leaves together, and made themselves aprons.*
>
> **Genesis 3:7**

Prior to this, Adam and Eve never needed to sew fig leaves together because God Himself provided their cover. ***Sometimes the realisation of nakedness is the evidence of departed glory***. It is a state where one toils - *works strenuously* - to meet material needs. Listen to what God says about toiling;

> *28Come unto me, all ye that labour and are heavy laden, and I will give you rest.*
>
> **Matthew 11:28**

Talking to many Christians today, the thought of self preservation far outweighs the restoration of glory. Jesus said in *Matthew 16*:

> *24Then said Jesus unto his disciples, If any man will come after me, let him deny himself, and take up his cross, and follow me.*
>
> *25FOR WHOSOEVER WILL SAVE HIS LIFE SHALL LOSE IT: AND WHOSOEVER WILL LOSE HIS LIFE FOR MY SAKE SHALL FIND IT.*
>
> *26For what is a man profited, if he shall gain the whole world, and lose his own soul? or what shall a man give in exchange for his soul?*
>
> **Matthew 16:24-26**

For many, the thought of loss overrides the ability to reproduce whatever is lost. The evidence that we are walking in faith is our ability to use it productively on demand; calling those things that are not as though they were.

Could it be that we hold on to things more than we need to because we fear we will not be able to recreate them the next time a need of them arises? God, our Father, knows what we need before we ask Him. If He feeds the birds surely He will feed and clothe us.

> *30Wherefore, if God so clothe the grass of the field, which to day is, and to morrow is cast into the oven, shall he not much more clothe you, O ye of little faith?*
>
> *31Therefore take no thought, saying, What shall we eat? or, What shall we drink? or, Wherewithal shall we be clothed?*
>
> *32(For after all these things do the Gentiles seek:) for your heavenly Father knoweth that ye have need of all these things.*

> *[33] But seek ye first the kingdom of God, and his righteousness; and all these things shall be added unto you.*
>
> *[34] Take therefore no thought for the morrow: for the morrow shall take thought for the things of itself. Sufficient unto the day is the evil thereof.*
>
> Matthew 6:30-34

This evil spirit causes people to kill their seed by planting the thought that a seed let go under the instruction of the Holy Spirit is a seed that diminishes you. The truth however is that the seed you let go is actually what increases you.

> *[24] There is that scattereth, and yet increaseth; and there is that withholdeth more than is meet, but it tendeth to poverty.*
>
> Proverbs 11:24

By the power of the Holy Spirit in us, we need to resist these devilish thoughts and they will flee. A mind focused on self-preservation cannot witness His power and glory. If we live our lives in the Spirit, we will not be consumed with self-preserving actions simply because we know that the Father's glory will cover *our nakedness*.

A miracle will always follow Godly wisdom

The rise of Self-Preservation

Ananias and Sapphira were part of the believers, after miracle of Pentecost in the early Church. During this time, we see certain wisdom in operation; this wisdom seems to elude the church in our time. There was singleness of heart at that time and those who had been blessed with possessions sold them to support those that did not have. There was no thought of self preservation.

> *[32] And the multitude of them that believed were of one heart and of one soul: neither said any of them that ought of the things which he possessed was his own; but they had all things common.*
>
> *[33] And with great power gave the apostles witness of the resurrection of the Lord Jesus: and great grace was upon them all.*

34Neither was there any among them that lacked: for as many as were possessors of lands or houses sold them, and brought the prices of the things that were sold,

35And laid them down at the apostles' feet: and distribution was made unto every man according as he had need.

36And Joses, who by the apostles was surnamed Barnabas, (which is, being interpreted, The son of consolation,) a Levite, and of the country of Cyprus,

37Having land, sold it, and brought the money, and laid it at the apostles' feet.

Acts 4:32-37

Though the disciples in this time of the church followed very unconventional wisdom, everyone's needs were met. Joses must have been a person of repute during that time for him to have been mentioned here. This wisdom does not only apply to the poor but the rich too. Some people who are already rich in things do not realise that it is through grace that God had allowed access to the things they have, even the notable followed the wisdom of God.

We do not need to resort to manipulation to get material resources for our needs to be met. A miracle will always follow Godly wisdom. When we follow the order of the kingdom, material things get added to us. This deceptive spirit has caused the church of Christ to believe we need to conform to the standards of the world in order to acquire material things.

The first act of toil in recorded history was when man made aprons to cover his nakedness. This first rule has influenced toil ever since. People toil for preservation – self preservation.

7

The spirit of the Sadducees promotes Earthly Wisdom

L ooking carefully at the story of Adam and Eve in the garden of Eden, we notice that the tree was called the tree of the knowledge of good and evil. We know that trees with fruits usually carry their seed in the fruit. We also know that where there is no law, there is no transgression. Therefore a law must be present before good and evil can be determined.

God's instruction to Adam was to prevent him from the *law of sin and death,* which could be accessed through the seed that was in the fruit of the tree of the knowledge of good and evil. God warned Adam that in the day he took of the fruit, he will surely die. This signifies that ***prior to Adam eating the fruit of this tree, he had no knowledge of good and evil or of the law of sin and death.*** This indicates that the intention for man was not for him to live by the knowledge of good and evil. Man was to be sustained by the voice of God in the garden.

> [16]*And the LORD God commanded the man, saying, Of every tree of the garden thou mayest freely eat:*
>
> [17]*But of the tree of the knowledge of good and evil, thou shalt not eat of it: for in the day that thou eatest thereof thou shalt surely die.*

Genesis 2:16-17

When Adam ate the fruit he died, as God had said, Adam no longer had access to the life of God. We need to understand that apart from "***the good***" and "***the evil***" there is also "***Life***". The knowledge of good and evil never leads to life. The knowledge of good and evil blocks our access to life. Though Adam had permission to access the tree of life, he never touched it. This implies that the nature of Adam, prior to the eating of the tree of the knowledge of good and evil, was not an eternal nature.

The eternal nature would have come from eating of the tree of life. After Adam had eaten the fruit of the tree of the knowledge of good and evil, he still had access to the tree of life until God blocked this access. But, why did God do this?

> *22And the LORD God said, Behold, the man is become as one of us, to know good and evil: AND NOW, LEST HE PUT FORTH HIS HAND, AND TAKE ALSO OF THE TREE OF LIFE, AND EAT, AND LIVE FOR EVER:*
>
> *23Therefore the LORD God sent him forth from the garden of Eden, to till the ground from whence he was taken.*
>
> *24So he drove out the man; and he placed at the east of the garden of Eden Cherubims, and a flaming sword which turned every way, to keep the way of the tree of life.*

Genesis 3:22-24

It was important for God to block the access to life because, had Adam been able to access it, he would have believed that it was his knowledge of good and evil that led him to life and immortality. That would have been wrong.

Human wisdom cannot create spiritual instructions.

The things of God come through spiritual instructions. Spiritual instructions are the words that proceed from God that cause miracles to happen in our situations. Spiritual instructions are not primarily determined by human wisdom, it requires spiritual insight. *Psalm 107:20* says *"He sent his word and healed them..."* It was not just the speaking of the word that healed them. It is the fact that the word spoken originated from God. Those who speak words that do not originate from God ultimately cause confusion in the Church.

We see an example of this in the story of the birth of Jesus, when Joseph discovered that Mary was pregnant.

> *18Now the birth of Jesus Christ was on this wise: When as his mother Mary was espoused to Joseph, before they came together, she was found with child of the Holy Ghost.*
>
> *19Then Joseph her husband, being a just man, and not willing to make her a public example, was minded to put her away privily.*

> *[20]But while he thought on these things, behold, the angel of the LORD appeared unto him in a dream, saying, Joseph, thou son of David, fear not to take unto thee Mary thy wife: for that which is conceived in her is of the Holy Ghost.*

Matthew 1:18-20

Joseph was preparing to do what was right according to the law of the time but through spiritual insight, he was able to do the "*life*" thing. Jesus referred to this type of spiritual insight when He asked His disciples about who the people said He was.

> *[13]When Jesus came into the coasts of Caesarea Philippi, he asked his disciples, saying, Whom do men say that I the Son of man am?*
>
> *[14]And they said, Some say that thou art John the Baptist: some, Elias; and others, Jeremias, or one of the prophets.*
>
> *[15]He saith unto them, But whom say ye that I am?*
>
> *[16]And Simon Peter answered and said, Thou art the Christ, the Son of the living God.*
>
> *[17]And Jesus answered and said unto him, Blessed art thou, Simon Barjona: for flesh and blood hath not revealed it unto thee, but my Father which is in heaven.*

Matthew 16:13-17

Jesus was stressing the need for insight that comes from God. This insight surpasses all human knowledge. This is one reason why Jesus said in *John 7:24*, "*Judge not according to appearance, but judge righteous judgement*". A believer that is not spiritual cannot obtain the kind of revelation Peter had here. This kind of insight should come naturally to every believer but too many believers are living in the realm of flesh and blood.

Human wisdom cannot create spiritual instructions. Spiritual instructions come from the Holy Spirit. However, human wisdom and intelligence can help translate spiritual instructions to actionable steps. For example, Peter and John said to the man at the gate called Beautiful in *Acts 3*, "*rise up and walk*". Of what value would that instruction have been if Peter had spoken in a language the man did not understand? It was the man's natural understanding of the instruction spoken that led to the action that brought about the miracle. Every spiritual instruction comes in clear, actionable words. It is never confusing.

Let us look at some spiritual instructions that Jesus gave:

> [1]*And it came to pass, that, as the people pressed upon him to hear the word of God, he stood by the lake of Gennesaret,*
>
> [2]*And saw two ships standing by the lake: but the fishermen were gone out of them, and were washing their nets.*
>
> [3]*And he entered into one of the ships, which was Simon's, and prayed him that he would thrust out a little from the land. And he sat down, and taught the people out of the ship.*
>
> [4]*Now when he had left speaking, he said unto Simon, Launch out into the deep, and let down your nets for a draught.*
>
> [5]*And Simon answering said unto him, Master, we have toiled all the night, and have taken nothing: nevertheless at thy word I will let down the net.*
>
> [6]*And when they had this done, they inclosed a great multitude of fishes: and their net brake.*
>
> [7]*And they beckoned unto their partners, which were in the other ship, that they should come and help them. And they came, and filled both the ships, so that they began to sink.*
>
> [8]*When Simon Peter saw it, he fell down at Jesus' knees, saying, Depart from me; for I am a sinful man, O Lord.*

Luke 5:1-8

Jesus' instruction to Peter was simple, "*Launch out into the deep and let down your nets for a draught.*" Peter had done this same thing all night without result. The release of the spiritual instruction brought instantaneous results. In another example, the spiritual instruction was *fill the waterpots with water* and *draw out now.*

> [1]*And the third day there was a marriage in Cana of Galilee; and the mother of Jesus was there:*
>
> [2]*And both Jesus was called, and his disciples, to the marriage.*
>
> [3]*And when they wanted wine, the mother of Jesus saith unto him, They have no wine.*
>
> [4]*Jesus saith unto her, Woman, what have I to do with thee? mine hour is not yet come.*
>
> [5]*His mother saith unto the servants, Whatsoever he saith unto you, do it.*
>
> [6]*And there were set there six waterpots of stone, after the manner of the purifying of the Jews, containing two or three firkins apiece.*
>
> [7]*Jesus saith unto them, Fill the waterpots with water. And they filled them up to the brim.*
>
> [8]*And he saith unto them, Draw out now, and bear unto the governor of the feast. And they bare it.*

⁹When the ruler of the feast had tasted the water that was made wine, and knew not whence it was: (but the servants which drew the water knew;) the governor of the feast called the bridegroom,

¹⁰And saith unto him, Every man at the beginning doth set forth good wine; and when men have well drunk, then that which is worse: but thou hast kept the good wine until now.

¹¹This beginning of miracles did Jesus in Cana of Galilee, and manifested forth his glory; and his disciples believed on him.

John 2: 1-11

After the instruction at this marriage, the results were also instantaneous. In each case, the instruction that Jesus gave was simple and direct, with no complicated interpretation service was required.

Results in the life of a believer are linked to the spiritual instructions they obey. The plan of the evil one is to prevent us from hearing spiritual instructions. The enemy knows that if he can stop the instruction, he will stop the miracle; hence the reason why he brings false doctrine. In *Genesis 3*, God blocked access to the way of the tree of life using a flaming sword and angels, but now God the Father, through Jesus, has given us access to that tree. Jesus declared Himself as the way, the truth and the life. He called Himself the door.

⁹I am the door: by me if any man enter in, he shall be saved, and shall go in and out, and find pasture.

John 10:9

The ONLY way to access the life of God is through Jesus. It is nonnegotiable. Good works or morally right thoughts will not lead to this life. It is the life that determines the pasture. Every promise of God is accessed through this life.

¹¹And this is the record, that God hath given to us eternal life, and this life is in his Son.

¹²He that hath the Son hath life; and he that hath not the Son of God hath not life.

¹³These things have I written unto you that believe on the name of the Son of God; that ye may know that ye have eternal life, and that ye may believe on the name of the Son of God.

1 John 5:11-13

Jesus is the express image of God the Father. The only means of salvation for the world. Jesus our Lamb has been slain once and will never be slain again. He entered once into the Holy of Holies and perfected all things.

8

The spirit of the Sadducees and Curses

*T*he spirit of the Sadducees attracts curses. Curses are spiritual and not natural. A curse restricts people to a state of unfruitfulness in specific areas. It also attracts negative circumstances or events into a person's life on a consistent basis. A curse will always result in a negative occurrence or state of being. {*It is important to note that it is not every negative occurrence that is a result of a curse*}. There are two primary ways by which curses are placed:

1. Curses by words

These are curses placed by the pronouncement of unfavourable words by the one cursing. These curses do not need any special invocation for them to be effective. In the olden days, they were written on a scroll. When this was not possible, it was enough for the curses to be uttered aloud and they possessed the power of self realisation. **This power of self realisation is not a characteristic of curses. It is a characteristic of words.** Words create a tangible equivalent of the thoughts they represent.

Curses were not restricted by distance. The words uttered are like a flying roll that found their way to the intended destination.

[1]Then I turned, and lifted up mine eyes, and looked, and behold a flying roll.

[2]And he said unto me, What seest thou? And I answered, I see a flying roll; the length thereof is twenty cubits, and the breadth thereof ten cubits.

[3]Then said he unto me, This is the curse that goeth forth over the face of the whole earth: for every one that stealeth shall be cut off as on this side according to it; and every one that sweareth shall be cut off as on that side according to it.

Zechariah 5:1-3

2. Curses by Choice

These are curses where a change of state or an unfavourable event occurs as a result of choices made by the believer. This kind of curse is caused when the believer does not listen to the voice of the Holy Spirit and ends up making the wrong choices. This curse is rooted in the spirit of the Sadducees.

> [19]*I call heaven and earth to record this day against you, that I HAVE SET BEFORE YOU LIFE AND DEATH, BLESSING AND CURSING: THEREFORE CHOOSE LIFE, that both thou and thy seed may live:*
>
> **Deuteronomy 30:19**

The curse of Adam and Eve in the Garden of Eden was a curse by choice not a curse by words. Their state did not change until Adam made a decision to eat of the fruit of the tree of knowledge of good and evil. Remember, in that same garden was the tree of life but for some reason Adam and Eve did not partake of its fruit.

Curses are sometimes considered outdated particularly in the *developed nations* and, even though it is not a word spoken about much in this day and age, lack of knowledge or understanding of curses does not make them unreal. Ignorance of the a law does not invalidate that law.

Words create a tangible equivalent of the thoughts they represent.

Two characteristics of curses that I have come to understand are that...

... Curses respect hierarchy

The *curser* can only curse someone lower than them; they cannot curse a higher being. In the battle of David and Goliath, Goliath cursed David by "his gods" as he spoke unfavourable words to David:

> [43]*And the Philistine said unto David, Am I a dog, that thou comest to me with staves? And the Philistine cursed David by his gods.*
>
> **1 Samuel 17:43**

We know the curse of Goliath had no effect on David because David killed him in a triumphant way, making it look too easy. I say to people searching for sophisticated weapons with which to overcome *their goliath*, just look for the *small stones;* they are equally as effective.

This is also true with blessing. The less is always blessed of the better. We cannot give what we do not have.

> *13For when God made promise to Abraham, because he could swear by no greater, he sware by himself,*
>
> *14Saying, Surely blessing I will bless thee, and multiplying I will multiply thee.*
>
> *15And so, after he had patiently endured, he obtained the promise.*
>
> *16For men verily swear by the greater: and an oath for confirmation is to them an end of all strife.*

Hebrews 6:13-16

All the people that blessed in the bible were greater than those they blessed and the blessing that was received manifested in a tangible form. Understanding the hierarchical nature of curses can bring a lot of comfort to the believer. The death and resurrection of Christ has brought us to a place where we are seated with Christ Jesus in heavenly places. As Christians we are redeemed from the curse of the law.

> *6And hath raised us up together, and made us sit together in heavenly places in Christ Jesus:*

Ephesians 2:6

From our position with Christ in heavenly places, there is no greater One or place. This makes it impossible for a believer to be cursed with this type of curse.

… Curses have generational consequences

Curses can have generational consequences because they affect the "seed" of the cursed. Any such curse of a generational nature, placed before salvation can be broken through knowledge and the anointing.

Many scriptures show the link between the curse and the seed. In the book of Genesis, immediately after Adam had eaten the fruit and God came into the garden looking for him, the seed was mentioned. In *Deuteronomy 30:19*, the seed was mentioned. In the story of Gehazi in *2 Kings 5:20-27*, the seed was mentioned.

The story of Gehazi, the servant of Elisha the prophet is one that shows a curse being placed for actions related to deception in financial matters through the operation of the spirit of the Sadducees.

Gehazi went after Naanam ignoring the wisdom of God through Elisha. When he came back, he attempted to deceive the man of God, but God in his infinite wisdom and knowledge revealed this to Elisha.

> [20]*But Gehazi, the servant of Elisha the man of God, said, Behold, my master hath spared Naaman this Syrian, in not receiving at his hands that which he brought: but, as the LORD liveth, I will run after him, and take somewhat of him.*
>
> [21]*So Gehazi followed after Naaman. And when Naaman saw him running after him, he lighted down from the chariot to meet him, and said, Is all well?*
>
> [22]*And he said, All is well. My master hath sent me, saying, Behold, even now there be come to me from mount Ephraim two young men of the sons of the prophets: give them, I pray thee, a talent of silver, and two changes of garments.*
>
> [23]*And Naaman said, Be content, take two talents. And he urged him, and bound two talents of silver in two bags, with two changes of garments, and laid them upon two of his servants; and they bare them before him.*
>
> [24]*And when he came to the tower, he took them from their hand, and bestowed them in the house: and he let the men go, and they departed.*
>
> [25]*But he went in, and stood before his master. And Elisha said unto him, Whence comest thou, Gehazi? And he said, Thy servant went no whither.*
>
> [26]*And he said unto him, Went not mine heart with thee, when the man turned again from his chariot to meet thee? Is it a time to receive money, and to receive garments, and oliveyards, and vineyards, and sheep, and oxen, and menservants, and maidservants?*
>
> [27]*The leprosy therefore of Naaman shall cleave unto thee, and unto thy seed for ever. And he went out from his presence a leper as white as snow.*

2 Kings 5:20-27

As believers, we need to know that this deception is real and can bring real consequences. Our ignorance of these things can stop us from getting the best of God even though Christ has redeemed us from the curse from the law, as stated in *Galatians 3:13*. Notice that Gehazi's seed was affected by this curse.

Another example is witnessed in the Garden of Eden.

> [14]*And the LORD God said unto the serpent, Because thou hast done this, thou art cursed above all cattle, and above every beast of the field; upon thy belly shalt thou go, and dust shalt thou eat all the days of thy life:*
>
> [15]*And I will put enmity between thee and the woman, and between thy seed and her seed; it shall bruise thy head, and thou shalt bruise his heel.*
>
> [16]*Unto the woman he said, I will greatly multiply thy sorrow and thy conception; in sorrow thou shalt bring forth children; and thy desire shall be to thy husband, and he shall rule over thee.*
>
> [17]*And unto Adam he said, Because thou hast hearkened unto the voice of thy wife, and hast eaten of the tree, of which I commanded thee, saying, Thou shalt not eat of it: cursed is the ground for thy sake; in sorrow shalt thou eat of it all the days of thy life;*
>
> [18]*Thorns also and thistles shall it bring forth to thee; and thou shalt eat the herb of the field;*
>
> [19]*In the sweat of thy face shalt thou eat bread, till thou return unto the ground; for out of it wast thou taken: for dust thou art, and unto dust shalt thou return.*

Genesis 3:14-19

Immediately after Adam ate the fruit, the ground was cursed for his sake. I had always read this as God cursing the ground because of Adam's sin, but the Holy Spirit gave me some insight.

God only told Adam what the state of the ground was as a result of his actions. God never curses us. It is our choices and actions that cause the state of things to change either favourably or otherwise. Notice it was the *ground* that had a changed state that led to all the other unfavourable things spoken about.

Why is this significant? When we read what Jesus had to say about the *ground* in *Matthew 13*, where Jesus spoke about seven mysteries of the kingdom, we see that each mystery bore within it the *resemblance* of something going below ground level.

9

The spirit of the Sadducees and the Mysteries of the Kingdom

B efore taking a look at the Mysteries of the Kingdom it is important to understand the concept of the "ground". Jesus said, *"If the seed does not fall into the ground and die, it abides alone"*. If we do not operate these mysteries concerning the seed God gives, God's power will not be able to work on it for the results we need.

> [24]*Verily, verily, I say unto you, Except a corn of wheat fall into the ground and die, it abideth alone: but if it die, it bringeth forth much fruit.*

> **John 12:24**

What is the Ground?

The *ground* represents the place where all natural desires die. It is the place we get to where natural wisdom and human understanding fail. It is amazing the number of people who had to face the deep pain of loss before seeing and understanding the path of true greatness. I wonder why the light always seems to be at the end of the tunnel.

> *His perfect will is discovered at the end of endurance and it takes God's wisdom to accept this*

The blessing of resurrection was hidden in the hill of crucifixion. As believers, we need to understand that Godly opportunities are hidden at the end of seasons of pain. Once the season is over and we enter into supernatural abundance, we start to experience the multiple mysteries of God.

The corn of wheat needs to stay long enough in the ground to die. We need to be careful that we do not pray ourselves out of the perfect will of God into his permissive will. Jesus avoided this.

> *⁴¹And he was withdrawn from them about a stone's cast, and kneeled down, and prayed,*
>
> *⁴²Saying, Father, if thou be willing, remove this cup from me: nevertheless not my will, but thine, be done.*
>
> *⁴³And there appeared an angel unto him from heaven, strengthening him.*
>
> *⁴⁴And being in an agony he prayed more earnestly: and his sweat was as it were great drops of blood falling down to the ground.*

Luke 22:41-44

His perfect will is discovered at the end of endurance and it takes God's wisdom to accept this. Jesus went through strong crying and tears in the days of His flesh. We are not greater than Him. Obedience is learnt through pain.

> *⁶As he saith also in another place, Thou art a priest for ever after the order of Melchisedec.*
>
> *⁷Who in the days of his flesh, when he had offered up prayers and supplications with strong crying and tears unto him that was able to save him from death, and was heard in that he feared;*
>
> *⁸Though he were a Son, yet learned he obedience by the things which he suffered;*
>
> *⁹And being made perfect, he became the author of eternal salvation unto all them that obey him;*
>
> *¹⁰Called of God an high priest after the order of Melchisedec.*

Hebrews 5:6-10

Be not deceived, entering into a place of rest will require us to contend in battle. Let us endure the pain and suffering; let us wait patiently for the will of God to have its full course. The end result is always good and provides everlasting joy. James the apostle encouraged us to count it all joy.

> *²My brethren, count it all joy when ye fall into divers temptations;*
>
> *³Knowing this, that the trying of your faith worketh patience.*
>
> *⁴But let patience have her perfect work, that ye may be perfect and entire, wanting nothing.*

James 1:2-4

We know all things work together for our good and our faith rests in the wisdom of God for deliverance. The challenges we face are the opportunities to apply these mysteries that the name of Jesus may be glorified.

Mysteries of the Kingdom

When I was younger, I heard the saying *"God works in mysterious ways"*. However, God's way is only a mystery to those who do not seek to understand Him, as it is given to believers to understand the mysteries of the kingdom. These mysteries show us the path to covenant dignity.

As believers, we do not control the seed, we control the environment. God gave us dominion over the environment and not the seed. It is God that gives the seed.

Taking hold of these mysteries transforms our lives beyond our imagination. They cause us to shine in a dark world. They help us convert toil to Godly labour. Let us look at these mysteries.

1. The Mystery of the Ground

This mystery is about the environment and not just the seed. It takes having good seed and good ground for a there to be a harvest. These two things were present in Eden. We use the mysteries of the kingdom in the atmosphere of His glory.

[3]And he spake many things unto them in parables, saying, Behold, a sower went forth to sow;

Matthew 13:3

The productive seeds were the ones that fell into the good ground. I have always wondered why this sower did not determine the state of the ground before sowing his seed. Sometimes, it is impossible to use human understanding to determine which experience or specific action will lead to results. *(Ecc 11:1-6)*

⁸But other fell into good ground, and brought forth fruit, some an hundredfold, some sixtyfold, some thirtyfold.

Matthew 13:8

All the seeds that fell into the ground in this story were good seed but they only produced results when the good seed landed in the good ground. As believers, we do not control the seed, we control the environment. God gave us dominion over the environment and not the seed. It is God that gives the seed.

¹⁰Now he that ministereth seed to the sower both minister bread for your food, and multiply your seed sown, and increase the fruits of your righteousness;)

2 Corinthians 9:10

2. The Mystery of Co-Existence

Have you ever wondered how the serpent got into the Garden of Eden, how satan was able to present himself before God concerning Job, or how Judas Iscariot was chosen as one of Jesus' twelve disciples?

²⁴Another parable put he forth unto them, saying, The kingdom of heaven is likened unto a man which sowed good seed in his field:

²⁵But while men slept, his enemy came and sowed tares among the wheat, and went his way.

²⁶But when the blade was sprung up, and brought forth fruit, then appeared the tares also

Matthew 13:24-26

³⁰Let both grow together until the harvest: and in the time of harvest I will say to the reapers, Gather ye together first the tares, and bind them in bundles to burn them: but gather the wheat into my barn.

Matthew 13:30

There are times when God in His wisdom and sovereignty allows *"negative influences"* into the camp. Initially it seems like victory for the enemy but God always has the last laugh as these influences are only used to achieve His purpose. Even though the spirit of the Sadducees seems to be infiltrating ranks within the church, be rest assured that God's perfect plan will definitely come to pass.

3. *The Mystery of the Seed.*

The mystery of the seed is the mystery of supernatural multiplication. Once we understand this mystery we can produce supernatural increase in the endeavours of our life. Increase based on sound knowledge and the application of Godly wisdom.

It is amazing how we tend to magnify what we do not have above the seed we do have. God is righteous and will never leave us seedless. God always places something in our hands; that something is our seed to greatness. He also gives us insight that ensures that the tiny seed becomes a mighty tree.

[31]Another parable put he forth unto them, saying, The kingdom of heaven is like to a grain of mustard seed, which a man took, and sowed in his field:

[32]Which indeed is the least of all seeds: but when it is grown, it is the greatest among herbs, and becometh a tree, so that the birds of the air come and lodge in the branches thereof.

Matthew 13:31-32

A lad's lunch was a seed for Jesus. He knew exactly what He was going to do with the seed before He did it and the results speak for themselves. The lad's lunch ends up feeding a multitude. A message was a seed for Peter and after listening to Peter's first message three thousand souls are saved.

4. *The Mystery of the Leaven.*

Jesus warned his disciples to beware of the leaven of the Pharisees and Sadducees. When he said this He referred to the doctrine of the Pharisees and Sadducees. These are deep rooted beliefs we hold concerning the application of things of the kingdom.

[33]Another parable spake he unto them; The kingdom of heaven is like unto leaven, which a woman took, and hid in three measures of meal, till the whole was leavened.

Matthew 13:33

The doctrines we bring into our lives are the ones that manifest in all areas. If we accept poverty in one area, it will quickly spread like a wild fire into other areas. This is one reason why the Scriptures say; "*take heed what you hear*". Once we hear something it opens up the possibility of meditation, which increases the probability of manifestation. The wrong message acted upon can abort your destiny.

[6]Then Jesus said unto them, Take heed and beware of the leaven of the Pharisees and of the Sadducees.

Matthew 16:6

5. *The Mystery of the Hidden Treasure.*

[44]Again, the kingdom of heaven is like unto treasure hid in a field; the which when a man hath found, he hideth, and for joy thereof goeth and selleth all that he hath, and buyeth that field.

Matthew 13:44

Have you ever asked yourself, *Why did this man not take the treasure and become rich?* He did not come back for the treasure; he came back for the field. Secondly the cost of the field was equal to the value of all he had. The price we need to pay for the things of the kingdom is always something we can afford.

Purpose in life is not in plurals. Double mindedness creates instability

---

Another thing to note is that the man hid the treasure. A lot of us leave our treasure in a place of contamination. Once the treasure is contaminated, it is devalued. Apostle Paul said, "*Evil communications corrupt good manners*". Any heavenly treasure exposed to and influenced by earthly wisdom is devalued. After Paul received his revelation he immediately refused to confer with flesh and blood or earthly wisdom. It took three years before he spoke to those that were apostles before him.

¹⁵*But when it pleased God, who separated me from my mother's womb, and called me by his grace,*

¹⁶*To reveal his Son in me, that I might preach him among the heathen; immediately I conferred not with flesh and blood:*

¹⁷*Neither went I up to Jerusalem to them which were apostles before me; but I went into Arabia, and returned again unto Damascus.*

¹⁸*Then after three years I went up to Jerusalem to see Peter, and abode with him fifteen days.*

¹⁹*But other of the apostles saw I none, save James the Lord's brother.*

Galatians 1:15-19

I pray God will open our eyes to see what we have in our hearts that can set us apart and cause us to be celebrated.

6.   The Mystery of the Hidden Pearl.

⁴⁵*Again, the kingdom of heaven is like unto a merchant man, seeking goodly pearls:*
⁴⁶*Who, when he had found one pearl of great price, went and sold all that he had, and bought it.*

Matthew 13:45-46

Valuable pearls are not found on the surface. They are found below ground level. This mystery almost sounds like that of the hidden treasure, but it is different. He sought pearls (*plural*) and found a pearl (*singular*). Purpose in life is not in plurals. Double mindedness creates instability. Once you find the pearl, the mystery of the seed kicks in. This mystery causes the single purpose to grow and meet every need. This single purpose will find multiple expressions.

7.   The Mystery of the Net.

The mystery of the net is one that is likened to one fishing.

⁴⁷*Again, the kingdom of heaven is like unto a net, that was cast into the sea, and gathered of every kind:*

⁴⁸*Which, when it was full, they drew to shore, and sat down, and gathered the good into vessels, but cast the bad away.*

Matthew 13:47-48

This mystery precedes the mystery of co-existence. It is this mystery that brings in Judas Iscariot. Notice that Jesus knew Judas was evil, yet he chose him.

> *⁷⁰Jesus answered them, Have not I chosen you twelve, and one of you is a devil?*
>
> *⁷¹He spake of Judas Iscariot the son of Simon: for he it was that should betray him, being one of the twelve.*

John 6:70-71

The presence of certain *unfavourable* circumstances enables you to see depths in God. It took a crucified Jesus to reveal a resurrected Christ and it required a possessed Judas to facilitate the process. This can only be the wisdom of God.

Finally, after confirming that the disciples understood what He had spoken concerning the mysteries, here is what Jesus said,

> *⁵¹Jesus saith unto them, Have ye understood all these things? They say unto him, Yea, Lord.*
>
> *⁵²Then said he unto them, Therefore every scribe which is instructed unto the kingdom of heaven is like unto a man that is an householder, which bringeth forth out of his treasure things new and old.*

Matthew 13:51-52

Once we understand the mysteries they become tools in our households. Everywhere in the book of Acts where the disciples required the use of these mysteries, the mysteries responded profitably to them. I pray that by reading this book, every one of these mysteries will become a tool in your hands and start to work for you, in the mighty name of Jesus.

10

The spirit of the Sadducees and Forms of Godliness

F orms of godliness are the natural works we engage ourselves in and the laws we institute in the name of God. These are laws which protect the institution more than the God the institution represents. These are the activities we think make us godly but in reality are a bondage to the people of God.

In the early church, a strong dispute arose as a result of such forms of godliness. God had done great works among the Gentiles and some men from Judea came to promote the circumcision of Moses as a requirement for salvation, trying to hold on to the message of salvation by works.

> *¹And certain men which came down from Judaea taught the brethren, and said, Except ye be circumcised after the manner of Moses, ye cannot be saved.*
>
> *²When therefore Paul and Barnabas had no small dissension and disputation with them, they determined that Paul and Barnabas, and certain other of them, should go up to Jerusalem unto the apostles and elders about this question.*
>
> *³And being brought on their way by the church, they passed through Phenice and Samaria, declaring the conversion of the Gentiles: and they caused great joy unto all the brethren.*
>
> *⁴And when they were come to Jerusalem, they were received of the church, and of the apostles and elders, and they declared all things that God had done with them.*
>
> *⁵But there rose up certain of the sect of the Pharisees which believed, saying, That it was needful to circumcise them, and to command them to keep the law of Moses.*

Acts 15:1-5

Prior to this, Barnabas and Paul had preached the message of salvation to the gentiles and many had given their lives to Christ: Signs and wonders had even happened (*Acts 14:1-3*). Now, these men must have occupied a position of authority for the people to have considered their words as authority. The fact that Paul and Barnabas could not convince them also proves they must have regarded Paul and Barnabas as peers, therefore prompting the need to go to Jerusalem, the seat of a higher authority.

This dispute continued in Jerusalem until Peter, a leader among the apostles and elders spoke.

> [7]*And when there had been much disputing, Peter rose up, and said unto them, Men and brethren, ye know how that a good while ago God made choice among us, that the Gentiles by my mouth should hear the word of the gospel, and believe.*
>
> [8]*And God, which knoweth the hearts, bare them witness, giving them the Holy Ghost, even as he did unto us;*
>
> [9]*And put no difference between us and them, purifying their hearts by faith.*
>
> [10]*Now therefore why tempt ye God, to put a yoke upon the neck of the disciples, which neither our fathers nor we were able to bear?*
>
> [11]*But we believe that through the grace of the LORD Jesus Christ we shall be saved, even as they.*
>
> [12]*Then all the multitude kept silence, and gave audience to Barnabas and Paul, declaring what miracles and wonders God had wrought among the Gentiles by them.*
>
> [13]*And after they had held their peace, James answered, saying, Men and brethren, hearken unto me:*
>
> [14]*Simeon hath declared how God at the first did visit the Gentiles, to take out of them a people for his name.*
>
> [15]*And to this agree the words of the prophets; as it is written,*
>
> [16]*After this I will return, and will build again the tabernacle of David, which is fallen down; and I will build again the ruins thereof, and I will set it up:*
>
> [17]*That the residue of men might seek after the Lord, and all the Gentiles, upon whom my name is called, saith the Lord, who doeth all these things.*
>
> [18]*Known unto God are all his works from the beginning of the world.*
>
> [19]*Wherefore my sentence is, that we trouble not them, which from among the Gentiles are turned to God:*
>
> [20]*But that we write unto them, that they abstain from pollutions of idols, and from fornication, and from things strangled, and from blood.*

Acts 15:7-20

The response was deliverance for the church among the gentiles. The yoke of a form of godliness was broken. When the gentiles heard the outcome of the dispute, they rejoiced for the consolation. The true gospel always brings consolation and joy. This situation is occurring again in the church, spirituality is being judged by involvement in religious activities that do not possess the power to deliver those that engage in them.

Without the involvement of the elders in Jerusalem and Paul and Barnabas having been there when these men came, the gentiles could have been misled about the true meaning and practice of Christianity. Christianity is not defined by religious activities. It is defined by transformation and impartation that can only occur when the spirit of man comes in contact with the Holy Spirit.

Christianity is not defined by religious activities. It is defined by transformation and impartation that can only occur when the spirit of man comes in contact with the Holy Spirit.

We as believers have not received the spirit of bondage again (*Rom 8:15*). We were delivered from darkness and have been translated into light, and the Spirit Himself bears witness with our spirits that we are children of God. Another example in scripture where misconceptions are broken is in the story of the outpouring of the Holy Spirit on the Gentiles.

[44]*While Peter yet spake these words, the Holy Ghost fell on all them which heard the word.*

[45]*And they of the circumcision which believed were astonished, as many as came with Peter, because that on the Gentiles also was poured out the gift of the Holy Ghost.*

[46]*For they heard them speak with tongues, and magnify God. Then answered Peter,*

[47]*Can any man forbid water, that these should not be baptized, which have received the Holy Ghost as well as we?*

[48]*And he commanded them to be baptized in the name of the Lord. Then prayed they him to tarry certain days.*

Acts 10:44-48

While Peter was preaching, the Holy Spirit fell on all that heard his word. This occurrence surprised the people because the gentiles had received the Holy Spirit without water baptism. *Verse 47* shows what was in the heart of Peter. If the Holy Spirit had not been poured on the Gentiles while Peter spoke, he probably would have recommended water baptism as a prerequisite for baptism in the Holy Ghost.

Over the last decade, the number of churches and church based organisations has risen. However, a significant number of these are not making the impact they should. A lot of believers think that once they are saved, everything changes and becomes new. This is true regarding the spirit of man, but the mind needs to be transformed (*Romans 12:1-2*). Notice that those who thought the yoke should be enforced among the elders in Jerusalem were of the sect of the Pharisees.

> *⁵But there rose up certain of the sect of the Pharisees which believed, saying, That it was needful to circumcise them, and to command them to keep the law of Moses.*

> Acts 15: 5

This indicates that some believers, though saved, may still possess minds that were trained by their past experiences and have not been washed with the water of the Word of God. This un-renewed mind keeps them in bondage to fear. Not only this, they will seek to bring those that are free under this same bondage. This is why our dependence on the Holy Spirit for spiritual interpretation of scripture cannot be over emphasised.

In talking about forms of godliness, I am not referring to the things that are categorically wrong according to the scriptures. I am talking about the things that are good but not right; things that are lawful but not expedient. Forms of godliness do not refer to the setting up of administrative offices in churches or organised groups.

> *¹This know also, that in the last days perilous times shall come.*
>
> *²For men shall be lovers of their own selves, covetous, boasters, proud, blasphemers, disobedient to parents, unthankful, unholy,*
>
> *³Without natural affection, trucebreakers, false accusers, incontinent, fierce, despisers of those that are good,*
>
> *⁴Traitors, heady, highminded, lovers of pleasures more than lovers of God;*
>
> *⁵Having a form of godliness, but denying the power thereof: from such turn away.*

> 2 Timothy 3:1-5

This is required. Jesus had an administrative organisation. Judas was responsible for the purse;

[29]For some of them thought, because Judas had the bag, that Jesus had said unto him, Buy those things that we have need of against the feast; or, that he should give something to the poor.

John 13:29

On many occasions, people made contact with the disciples before getting to Jesus. We will always need people to help with the handling of the multitude and some people in the Church are specifically anointed to provide this kind of service.

[28]And God hath set some in the church, first apostles, secondarily prophets, thirdly teachers, after that miracles, then gifts of healings, HELPS, GOVERNMENTS, diversities of tongues.

1 Corinthians 12:28

Believers need to realise that the ministry of helps and governments are also anointed ministries in the church. It takes an anointing to be able to serve effectively when the mysteries of the kingdom of God are in operation. For example, what training did the disciples have to be able to organise and feed five thousand men, besides women and children, in a meeting that was not preplanned? How did they coordinate the seating arrangements, the distribution of the food and the collection of the remaining fragments? Jesus did not tell them what He was going to do. In this day and age *wisdom* would have to be applied before considering such.

The apostles in the book of Acts had a situation that completely depicts this. The disciples had to organise so they could handle the growth of the church, and the murmuring that came along with that.

[1]And in those days, when the number of the disciples was multiplied, there arose a murmuring of the Grecians against the Hebrews, because their widows were neglected in the daily ministration.

[2]Then the twelve called the multitude of the disciples unto them, and said, It is not reason that we should leave the word of God, and serve tables.

[3]Wherefore, brethren, look ye out among you seven men of honest report, full of the Holy Ghost and wisdom, whom we may appoint over this business.

[4]But we will give ourselves continually to prayer, and to the ministry of the word.

[5]And the saying pleased the whole multitude: and they chose Stephen, a man full of

> faith and of the Holy Ghost, and Philip, and Prochorus, and Nicanor, and Timon, and Parmenas, and Nicolas a proselyte of Antioch:
>
> *⁶Whom they set before the apostles: and when they had prayed, they laid their hands on them.*
>
> *⁷And the word of God increased; and the number of the disciples multiplied in Jerusalem greatly; and a great company of the priests were obedient to the faith.*
>
> Acts 6:1-7

The twelve said, *It is not good to leave the word of God and serve tables.* Notice that they looked for people they could trust and put them in charge of this business. Though the work of God is not a business, i.e. not for profit, it is still the Master's business. The operations of the administrative office should be run in a business minded manner in terms of the acquisition and allocation of resources. This however refers specifically to the ministry related expression. There are other expressions of the kingdom that are profit making. Commercial businesses should be profit making.

The formation of this group of seven is *a form of godliness* that is required. The apostles were careful to ensure that the management of the business did not overshadow the ministry of the word. It is this ministry of the Word that creates the business.

Verse 7 tells says it all, "*And the word of God increased and the disciples multiplied...*" Some organisations are not growing simply because "*the seven*" have not been appointed.

It is the ministry, not the business that makes the difference

Sometimes a ministry can have so many efficient processes that people begin to think that it is the processes that make the difference and they start to trust in these processes. It is effective ministry that gives birth to efficient processes, not the other way round. Let us look at Paul's instruction in 1 Corinthians:

> *¹And I, brethren, when I came to you, came not with excellency of speech or of wisdom, declaring unto you the testimony of God.*
>
> *²For I determined not to know any thing among you, save Jesus Christ, and him*

crucified.

³And I was with you in weakness, and in fear, and in much trembling.

⁴And my speech and my preaching was not with enticing words of man's wisdom, but in demonstration of the Spirit and of power:

⁵That your faith should not stand in the wisdom of men, but in the power of God.

⁶Howbeit we speak wisdom among them that are perfect: yet not the wisdom of this world, nor of the princes of this world, that come to nought:

⁷But we speak the wisdom of God in a mystery, even the hidden wisdom, which God ordained before the world unto our glory:

⁸Which none of the princes of this world knew: for had they known it, they would not have crucified the Lord of glory.

1 Corinthians 2:1-8

The focus of the kingdom is always on the power of God and not the wisdom of men. Sometimes, when organisations get to a point of great increase, a lot of wastage is introduced. There is nothing God provides that does not have a purpose and assignment.

Look at how Jesus responded to increase after a manifestation of the mystery of the mustard seed.

¹After these things Jesus went over the sea of Galilee, which is the sea of Tiberias.

²And a great multitude followed him, because they saw his miracles which he did on them that were diseased.

³And Jesus went up into a mountain, and there he sat with his disciples.

⁴And the passover, a feast of the Jews, was nigh.

⁵When Jesus then lifted up his eyes, and saw a great company come unto him, he saith unto Philip, Whence shall we buy bread, that these may eat?

⁶And this he said to prove him: for he himself knew what he would do.

⁷Philip answered him, Two hundred pennyworth of bread is not sufficient for them, that every one of them may take a little.

⁸One of his disciples, Andrew, Simon Peter's brother, saith unto him,

⁹There is a lad here, which hath five barley loaves, and two small fishes: but what are they among so many?

¹⁰And Jesus said, Make the men sit down. Now there was much grass in the place. So the men sat down, in number about five thousand.

¹¹And Jesus took the loaves; and when he had given thanks, he distributed to the disciples, and the disciples to them that were set down; and likewise of the fishes as much as they would.

> [12]*When they were filled, he said unto his disciples, Gather up the fragments that remain, that nothing be lost.*

John 6:1-12

Jesus specifically instructed the disciples to *gather up the fragments that remain*. Abundance is no excuse for wastage.

11

Other Signs of the spirit of the Sadducees

*I*t is the will of God for us to use the mysteries of the kingdom profitably. He wants our profiting to appear to all. The results of our believing and speaking should be apparent to all. There should always be a physical manifestation when we walk in faith.

> *[4]And my speech and my preaching was not with enticing words of man's wisdom, but in demonstration of the Spirit and of power:*
>
> *[5]That your faith should not stand in the wisdom of men, but in the power of God.*

1 Corinthians 2:4-5

> *[20]For the kingdom of God is not in word, but in power.*

1 Corinthians 4:20

Can you imagine how painful and frustrating it would have been if all Jesus did was talk, and no signs and wonders were recorded in the bible?

The early church exploded because the people heard the word of God and saw the miracles that followed. The preaching was not based on *words today, signs tomorrow*. As the people heard the word of God, they saw real miracles. There are a number of pointers to the operation of the spirit of the Sadducees in addition to the ones already talked about. Let us look some other areas.

> *[5]Then Philip went down to the city of Samaria, and preached Christ unto them.*
>
> *[6]And the people with one accord gave heed unto those things which Philip spake, hearing and seeing the miracles which he did.*
>
> *[7]For unclean spirits, crying with loud voice, came out of many that were possessed with them: and many taken with palsies, and that were lame, were healed.*
>
> *[8]And there was great joy in that city.*

Acts 8:5-8

The manifestation of the Spirit is limited

Limited manifestations of the Spirit is not the plan of God. It is God's desire for the manifestation of the Spirit to become an integral part of our lives. We cannot live a profitable life without the Holy Spirit.

When this evil spirit is in operation, tradition, methods and socially acceptable programs are magnified above the Word of God.

The spirit of the Sadducees plays down the operation of the gifts of the Spirit. This evil spirit tends to deny the operation of spiritual gifts. Paul did not want the church at Corinth to be ignorant of these spiritual things:

> [1]*Now concerning spiritual gifts, brethren, I would not have you ignorant.*
>
> [2]*Ye know that ye were Gentiles, carried away unto these dumb idols, even as ye were led.*
>
> [3]*Wherefore I give you to understand, that no man speaking by the Spirit of God calleth Jesus accursed: and that no man can say that Jesus is the Lord, but by the Holy Ghost.*
>
> [4]*Now there are diversities of gifts, but the same Spirit.*
>
> [5]*And there are differences of administrations, but the same Lord.*
>
> [6]*And there are diversities of operations, but it is the same God which worketh all in all.*
>
> [7]*But the manifestation of the Spirit is given to every man to profit withal.*
>
> [8]*For to one is given by the Spirit the word of wisdom; to another the word of knowledge by the same Spirit;*
>
> [9]*To another faith by the same Spirit; to another the gifts of healing by the same Spirit;*
>
> [10]*To another the working of miracles; to another prophecy; to another discerning of spirits; to another divers kinds of tongues; to another the interpretation of tongues:*
>
> [11]*But all these worketh that one and the selfsame Spirit, dividing to every man severally as he will.*

1 Corinthians 12:1-11

When this evil spirit is in operation, tradition, methods and socially acceptable programs are magnified above the Word of God. There are so many steps that are being given as prescriptions for getting the spiritual and an attempt to follow most of these prescriptions quickly reveals a missing step which breeds frustration. Access to the spiritual should not be based on trial and error. In most gatherings of believers today, the manifestation of the gifts are either absent or reserved for the chosen few but every believer has access to these gifts.

> [26]*How is it then, brethren? when ye come together, every one of you hath a psalm, hath a doctrine, hath a tongue, hath a revelation, hath an interpretation. Let all things be done unto edifying.*
>
> [27]*If any man speak in an unknown tongue, let it be by two, or at the most by three, and that by course; and let one interpret.*
>
> [28]*But if there be no interpreter, let him keep silence in the church; and let him speak to himself, and to God.*
>
> [29]*Let the prophets speak two or three, and let the other judge.*
>
> [30]*If any thing be revealed to another that sitteth by, let the first hold his peace.*
>
> [31]*For ye may all prophesy one by one, that all may learn, and all may be comforted.*
>
> [32]*And the spirits of the prophets are subject to the prophets.*
>
> [33]*For God is not the author of confusion, but of peace, as in all churches of the saints.*

1 Corinthians 14:26-33

Apostle Paul tells believers what to do when they come together in meetings. There were diversities of manifestations coming from different people and these manifestations were not just the gifts of the Spirit. Paul spoke about other manifestations such as a *psalm*, a *doctrine*, a *tongue*, a *revelation* and an *interpretation*. Paul also indicated that they were not reserved for the few. He cautioned the believers about doing this orderly, which implies that more than a few wanted to do this. In the letter to the Ephesians, Paul describes the scene more graphically.

> [18]*And be not drunk with wine, wherein is excess; but be filled with the Spirit;*
>
> [19]*Speaking to yourselves in psalms and hymns and spiritual songs, singing and making melody in your heart to the Lord;*
>
> [20]*Giving thanks always for all things unto God and the Father in the name of our Lord Jesus Christ,*
>
> [21]*Submitting yourselves one to another in the fear of God.*

Ephesians 5:18-21

Paul compares being filled with the Spirit to the intoxication of wine. Many believers in the church today are too dignified for the Holy Spirit to manifest through them, and I am not referring to the excesses we sometimes see. These excesses are things that right teaching will eliminate. Many would rather preserve personal dignity than be used by the Holy Spirit. We should not stop the use of a good thing completely because it has been abused.

Ignorance will be healed through the outburst of divinely inspired teaching that will pierce the spirit of the Sadducees.

Psalms are not things of the past. Doctrines need to be expounded so believers can be rooted and grounded in the knowledge of God. Revelation, tongues and interpretations are needed for the edification, exhortation and comforting of the body. When the church was together in a place, they were not just speaking in tongues. In fact Paul says, "Will the unlearned not say you are mad?" Tongues are not for public show except there is interpretation.

> [23]*If therefore the whole church be come together into one place, and all speak with tongues, and there come in those that are unlearned, or unbelievers, will they not say that ye are mad?*
>
> [24]*But if all prophesy, and there come in one that believeth not, or one unlearned, he is convinced of all, he is judged of all:*
>
> [25]*And thus are the secrets of his heart made manifest; and so falling down on his face he will worship God, and report that God is in you of a truth.*
>
> [26]*How is it then, brethren? when ye come together, every one of you hath a psalm, hath a doctrine, hath a tongue, hath a revelation, hath an interpretation. Let all things be done unto edifying.*

1 Corinthians 14:23-26

Prophetic utterances that reveal the secrets of the heart are evidence for the unbeliever that God is at work in us. It is almost the acceptable order now for people in the church to hold programs similar to that of unbelievers in a bid to attract them to church. Some of these events descend so low that it is sometimes difficult to tell if it is a Christian event or not. If attendance is high and ratings are high then we are successful but do these things define success? True transformation requires the

Holy Spirit. The manifestation of the gifts is available through us to cause lasting change.

I remember a meeting many years back in Nigeria. In the middle of a worship service, a few seconds before someone walked into the meeting room, the electricity supply was cut off. As this person walked in, the brother leading the service called out the name of the person and told him everything he had thought about from the time he left home till the time he arrived at the meeting. The level of accuracy was shocking. In another meeting, I remember that the person leading called a sister out and with shocking accuracy told her about a situation that occurred at her place of work earlier that day. In these two testimonies God brought mighty deliverance and comfort to the people involved.

Prayer is not the solution for ignorance. The cure for ignorance is right teaching.

Ignorance in spiritual things coupled with tradition has pushed back the operation of the Spirit in the church. This is changing with the change in dispensation to power and glory. Ignorance will be healed through the outburst of divinely inspired teaching that will pierce the spirit of the Sadducees.

[1]Then came together unto him the Pharisees, and certain of the scribes, which came from Jerusalem.

[2]And when they saw some of his disciples eat bread with defiled, that is to say, with unwashen, hands, they found fault.

[3]For the Pharisees, and all the Jews, except they wash their hands oft, eat not, holding the tradition of the elders.

[4]And when they come from the market, except they wash, they eat not. And many other things there be, which they have received to hold, as the washing of cups, and pots, brasen vessels, and of tables.

[5]Then the Pharisees and scribes asked him, Why walk not thy disciples according to the tradition of the elders, but eat bread with unwashen hands?

[6]He answered and said unto them, Well hath Esaias prophesied of you hypocrites, as it is written, This people honoureth me with their lips, but their heart is far from me.

[7]Howbeit in vain do they worship me, teaching for doctrines the commandments of

men.

[8]For laying aside the commandment of God, ye hold the tradition of men, as the washing of pots and cups: and many other such like things ye do.

[9]And he said unto them, Full well ye reject the commandment of God, that ye may keep your own tradition.

[10]For Moses said, Honour thy father and thy mother; and, Whoso curseth father or mother, let him die the death:

[11]But ye say, If a man shall say to his father or mother, It is Corban, that is to say, a gift, by whatsoever thou mightest be profited by me; he shall be free.

[12]And ye suffer him no more to do ought for his father or his mother;

[13]Making the word of God of none effect through your tradition, which ye have delivered: and many such like things do ye.

[14]And when he had called all the people unto him, he said unto them, Hearken unto me every one of you, and understand:

Mark 7:1-14

Prayer is not the solution for ignorance. The cure for ignorance is right teaching. A tradition is an institutionalised set of beliefs, thoughts and actions rooted in natural wisdom. These human thoughts and teachings seem right and acceptable but they shield minds from the illumination of the gospel, making the Word of God of no effect. This does not mean that the Word of God loses its power. It simply means the person that needs the Word of God is held in a position of restraint.

We see an example of this on one occasion when Jesus wanted to do great works but the unbelief in the people, caused by the traditions, hindered Him. The situation is no different today.

[1]And he went out from thence, and came into his own country; and his disciples follow him.

[2]And when the sabbath day was come, he began to teach in the synagogue: and many hearing him were astonished, saying, From whence hath this man these things? and what wisdom is this which is given unto him, that even such mighty works are wrought by his hands?

[3]Is not this the carpenter, the son of Mary, the brother of James, and Joses, and of Juda, and Simon? and are not his sisters here with us? And they were offended at him.

[4]But Jesus, said unto them, A prophet is not without honour, but in his own country, and among his own kin, and in his own house.

[5]And he could there do no mighty work, save that he laid his hands upon a few sick

folk, and healed them.

⁶And he marvelled because of their unbelief. And he went round about the villages, teaching.

Jesus wanted to do mighty works but He could not. After marvelling at their unbelief, He immediately went round the villages *teaching*. I believe Jesus had to go around teaching so as to increase the level of understanding and faith in the people. While doing this, He must have noticed that the work was great so He empowered the disciples to do the same things He was doing:

⁷And he called unto him the twelve, and began to send them forth by two and two; and gave them power over unclean spirits;

Mark 6:7

¹²And they went out, and preached that men should repent.

¹³And they cast out many devils, and anointed with oil many that were sick, and healed them.

Mark 6:12-13

Initially, it was only a few sick folk that could be healed. After this intensified level of teaching, many demons were cast out and many that were sick were healed. The combination of diligent study of the scriptures, effectual fervent prayer and fasting unlocks the flow of power. Mentally agreeing to the reality of the Word of God is not enough. The revelation of the true Christ is born in the place of travail. Paul the apostle spoke about a travail that leads to the formation of Christ in us.

¹⁹My little children, of whom I travail in birth again until Christ be formed in you,

Galatians 4:19

Another example of where unbelief hindered the operation of the power of God is seen in the gospel according to Matthew;

¹⁴And when they were come to the multitude, there came to him a certain man, kneeling down to him, and saying,

¹⁵Lord, have mercy on my son: for he is lunatick, and sore vexed: for ofttimes he falleth into the fire, and oft into the water.

> ¹⁶*And I brought him to thy disciples, and they could not cure him.*
>
> ¹⁷*Then Jesus answered and said, O faithless and perverse generation, how long shall I be with you? how long shall I suffer you? bring him hither to me.*
>
> ¹⁸*And Jesus rebuked the devil; and he departed out of him: and the child was cured from that very hour.*
>
> ¹⁹*Then came the disciples to Jesus apart, and said, Why could not we cast him out?*
>
> ²⁰*And Jesus said unto them, Because of your unbelief: for verily I say unto you, If ye have faith as a grain of mustard seed, ye shall say unto this mountain, Remove hence to yonder place; and it shall remove; and nothing shall be impossible unto you.*
>
> ²¹*Howbeit this kind goeth not out but by prayer and fasting.*

Matthew 17:14-21

I once heard a man of God say concerning this scripture, "If Jesus had not been there, the disciples would most likely have said it was not the will of God for the boy to be healed". **Most delayed miracles are as a result of insufficient faith and not a lack of willingness on God's part.** Unfortunately a lot of people do not accept the *unbelief* side of the equation. It is far easier to blame the willingness side as this is easier on the ego.

If we humble ourselves and turn to God, great works beyond our imagination will manifest in our time.

Incomplete Teaching of the Word of God

Incomplete teaching is another sign of this spirit. This is the teaching of salvation without the baptism of the Holy Spirit, it is the teaching of healing without divine health. In order for the word of God to work, we need to have spiritual understanding through revelation from the Holy Spirit. A lot of teaching around today appeals to the mind. It is too politically correct; it lacks the power to penetrate the depths of the heart.

> ¹²*For the word of God is quick, and powerful, and sharper than any twoedged sword, piercing even to the dividing asunder of soul and spirit, and of the joints and marrow, and is a discerner of the thoughts and intents of the heart.*

Hebrews 4:12

The preaching and teaching of the word of God always produces joy and amazement when accompanied by signs. These signs confirm the spoken Word. A lot of believers are not seeing signs and miracles because they are not hearing the right teaching.

> [26] *And they were all amazed, and they glorified God, and were filled with fear, saying, We have seen strange things to day.*

Luke 5:26

Many miracles accompanied Jesus but a large number took place after teaching or preaching the Word of God.

> [17] *And it came to pass on a certain day, as he was teaching, that there were Pharisees and doctors of the law sitting by, which were come out of every town of Galilee, and Judaea, and Jerusalem: and the power of the Lord was present to heal them.*
> [18] *And, behold, men brought in a bed a man which was taken with a palsy: and they sought means to bring him in, and to lay him before him.*

Luke 5:17-18

Incomplete teaching of the word of God robs a lot of believers of the manifestation of the Spirit. The story of Apollos in *Acts 18* shows the effect of this incomplete teaching. God has placed teachers in the church. These are people who are anointed for spiritual insight into the word of God. They bring simple understanding to hidden mysteries.

> [24] *And a certain Jew named Apollos, born at Alexandria, an eloquent man, and mighty in the scriptures, came to Ephesus.*
> [25] *This man was instructed in the way of the Lord; and being fervent in the spirit, he spake and taught diligently the things of the Lord, knowing only the baptism of John.*
> [26] *And he began to speak boldly in the synagogue: whom when Aquila and Priscilla had heard, they took him unto them, and expounded unto him the way of God more perfectly.*

Acts 18:24-26

This eloquent man, mighty in scripture, went to Ephesus and taught the people in the synagogue. Apollos had been instructed in the way of the Lord and all he knew was the baptism of John. John's baptism was only repentance and of the kingdom of God.

~ 69 ~

> [11]*I indeed baptize you with water unto repentance. but he that cometh after me is mightier than I, whose shoes I am not worthy to bear: he shall baptize you with the Holy Ghost, and with fire:*

Matthew 3:11

The people in Ephesus had only been exposed to John's message. They were missing out on the Holy Spirit and fire part. In these last days, we need the Holy Spirit and fire more than ever. When Aquila and Priscilla heard him, in the spirit of love, they explained the way of God more perfectly. The impact of this incomplete teaching is what is important here. Following the sessions with Aquila and Priscilla, Apollos moved to Corinth. Apostle Paul coming to Ephesus found certain disciples who he questioned about the Holy Spirit but they had not heard anything about the Holy Spirit. The knowledge of the baptism of John was all they knew.

The anointing only works where you have been sent and not where there is a need.

There are a lot of people in the Church today who, like these early Christians, only have a limited understanding of the word of God due to incomplete teaching. *Acts 19* shows the results of the teaching of Christ:

> [1]*And it came to pass, that, while Apollos was at Corinth, Paul having passed through the upper coasts came to Ephesus: and finding certain disciples,*
>
> [2]*He said unto them, Have ye received the Holy Ghost since ye believed? And they said unto him, We have not so much as heard whether there be any Holy Ghost.*
>
> [3]*And he said unto them, Unto what then were ye baptized? And they said, Unto John's baptism.*
>
> [4]*Then said Paul, John verily baptized with the baptism of repentance, saying unto the people, that they should believe on him which should come after him, that is, on Christ Jesus.*
>
> [5]*When they heard this, they were baptized in the name of the Lord Jesus.*
>
> [6]*And when Paul had laid his hands upon them, the Holy Ghost came on them; and they spake with tongues, and prophesied.*
>
> [7]*And all the men were about twelve.*
>
> [8]*And he went into the synagogue, and spake boldly for the space of three months, disputing and persuading the things concerning the kingdom of God.*

⁹*But when divers were hardened, and believed not, but spake evil of that way before the multitude, he departed from them, and separated the disciples, disputing daily in the school of one Tyrannus.*

¹⁰*And this continued by the space of two years; so that all they which dwelt in Asia heard the word of the Lord Jesus, both Jews and Greeks.*

¹¹*And God wrought special miracles by the hands of Paul:*

¹²*So that from his body were brought unto the sick handkerchiefs or aprons, and the diseases departed from them, and the evil spirits went out of them.*

Acts 19:1-12

Paul, by the help of the Holy Spirit, explained the true Christ to these people and laid hands on them that they might receive the Holy Spirit. Following this encounter, there was an instant manifestation of the Holy Spirit and the people prophesied.

The anointing is triggered when an instruction from God is obeyed.

Paul faced massive opposition to the teaching of the word. Those who were grounded in the teaching of the baptism of John had suddenly lost relevance because a change in dispensation had come. Many rejected Paul's message and there needed to be a separation of the disciples. This teaching continued for two years and special miracles followed. Prior to this, there were no *special miracles*!

The temptation to prove Sonship with signs

As we get bolder in our declaration of the gospel, we will be asked for signs to prove our sonship. We need to resist this temptation. Jesus had just completed forty days and nights of fasting and He was hungry before satan tempted him by asking Him to turn stones to bread.

¹*The Pharisees also with the Sadducees came, and tempting desired him that he would shew them a sign from heaven.*

Matthew 16:1

> *[3]And when the tempter came to him, he said, If thou be the Son of God, command that these stones be made bread.*

Matthew 4:3

Though this requirement for food was a legitimate one by human standards, Jesus resisted the temptation;

> *[4]And Jesus answered him, saying, It is written, That man shall not live by bread alone, but by every word of God.*

Luke 4:4

While reading this scripture I realised that the need does not trigger the anointing. The anointing is triggered when an instruction from God is obeyed. There were many widows in the days of Elisha but he was only sent to one. There were many apostles, but Peter was sent to Cornelius and Paul was sent to the Gentiles. The anointing only works where you have been sent and not where there is a need. If there is no leading, there will be no miracle. It is those that are led by the Spirit that are Sons. In the first Epistle to Timothy, Paul says, "*Lay hands suddenly on no man*". Consistent attempts to get miracles without the inspired Word of God can diminish our faith.

In the last days, we expect an unprecedented number of Christians to walk in the power of God. Many will enter into the reality of sonship. This reality will bring along a flow of the supernatural in a dimension that the world has never seen.

> *[19]For the earnest expectation of the creature waiteth for the manifestation of the sons of God.*

Romans 8:19

> *[11]But if the Spirit of him that raised up Jesus from the dead dwell in you, he that raised up Christ from the dead shall also quicken your mortal bodies by his Spirit that dwelleth in you.*

Romans 8:11

These works will exceed the ones Jesus did while He was on earth.

> [12]*Verily, verily, I say unto you, He that believeth on me, the works that I do shall he do also; and greater works than these shall he do; because I go unto my Father*

> **John 14:12**

The purpose of signs and wonders is to confirm the Word of God. A miracle occurs because a need exists for which a heart's cry has gone up to God and a word has been sent from above. It is this sent word that produces the physical manifestation we see. Here is an example from the scriptures:

> [23]*And being let go, they went to their own company, and reported all that the chief priests and elders had said unto them.*

> [24]*And when they heard that, they lifted up their voice to God with one accord, and said, Lord, thou art God, which hast made heaven, and earth, and the sea, and all that in them is:*

> [25]*Who by the mouth of thy servant David hast said, Why did the heathen rage, and the people imagine vain things?*

> [26]*The kings of the earth stood up, and the rulers were gathered together against the Lord, and against his Christ.*

> [27]*For of a truth against thy holy child Jesus, whom thou hast anointed, both Herod, and Pontius Pilate, with the Gentiles, and the people of Israel, were gathered together,*

> [28]*For to do whatsoever thy hand and thy counsel determined before to be done.*

> [29]*And now, Lord, behold their threatenings: and grant unto thy servants, that with all boldness they may speak thy word,*

> [30]*By stretching forth thine hand to heal; and that signs and wonders may be done by the name of thy holy child Jesus.*

> [31]*And when they had prayed, the place was shaken where they were assembled together; and they were all filled with the Holy Ghost, and they spake the word of God with boldness.*

> **Acts 4:23-31**

> [12]*And by the hands of the apostles were many signs and wonders wrought among the people; (and they were all with one accord in Solomon's porch.*

> **Acts 5:12**

In the gospel according to Mark, the instruction from Jesus was to preach the message of the kingdom first, and then the signs will follow. The signs being an indication of approval from God (*Acts 2:22*)

> [15]*And he said unto them, Go ye into all the world, and preach the gospel to every*

creature.

[16]He that believeth and is baptized shall be saved; but he that believeth not shall be damned.

[17]And these signs shall follow them that believe; In my name shall they cast out devils; they shall speak with new tongues;

[18]They shall take up serpents; and if they drink any deadly thing, it shall not hurt them; they shall lay hands on the sick, and they shall recover.

[19]So then after the Lord had spoken unto them, he was received up into heaven, and sat on the right hand of God.

[20]And they went forth, and preached every where, the Lord working with them, and confirming the word with signs following. Amen.

Mark 16:15-20

The signs always confirm the Word of God. When we start walking in this dimension of the Holy Spirit, the *testimony of men* is not that important.

Miracles are used to confirm scriptures and not to obtain testimony from men.

Why is it important to reject the testimony of men?

Jesus was careful not to accept the testimony of men because it would have given the Pharisees and the Sadducees the right to pronounce confirmation on His ministry. This would have meant that the people would have taken the Pharisees and Sadducees as the confirming authority. Jesus did not require this and neither do we.

[30]I can of mine own self do nothing: as I hear, I judge: and my judgment is just; because I seek not mine own will, but the will of the Father which hath sent me.

[31]If I bear witness of myself, my witness is not true.

[32]There is another that beareth witness of me; and I know that the witness which he witnesseth of me is true.

[33]Ye sent unto John, and he bare witness unto the truth.

[34]But I receive not testimony from man: but these things I say, that ye might be saved.

[35]He was a burning and a shining light: and ye were willing for a season to rejoice in his light.

[36]But I have greater witness than that of John: for the works which the Father hath given me to finish, the same works that I do, bear witness of me, that the Father hath

sent me.

37And the Father himself, which hath sent me, hath borne witness of me. Ye have neither heard his voice at any time, nor seen his shape.

38And ye have not his word abiding in you: for whom he hath sent, him ye believe not.

39Search the scriptures; for in them ye think ye have eternal life: and they are they which testify of me.

40And ye will not come to me, that ye might have life.

41I receive not honour from men.

John 5:30-41

Jesus was clear on where the testimony should originate from. He told them to search the Scriptures, therein lies the word that will confirm the authenticity of our works. Take a look a Jesus' response when John the Baptist sent his disciples to ask Him if He was He who is to come:

19And John calling unto him two of his disciples sent them to Jesus, saying, Art thou he that should come? or look we for another?

20When the men were come unto him, they said, John Baptist hath sent us unto thee, saying, Art thou he that should come? or look we for another?

21And in that same hour he cured many of their infirmities and plagues, and of evil spirits; and unto many that were blind he gave sight.

22Then Jesus answering said unto them, Go your way, and tell John what things ye have seen and heard; how that the blind see, the lame walk, the lepers are cleansed, the deaf hear, the dead are raised, to the poor the gospel is preached.

23And blessed is he, whosoever shall not be offended in me.

Luke 7:19-23

This response was quite interesting. In the same hour of the question, Jesus did some things and told John's disciples to go and tell John what they had seen and heard. However, when we take a closer look at what happened here and the words that Jesus had spoken earlier on, we realise that He only confirmed scriptures.

Miracles are used to confirm scriptures and not to obtain testimony from men.

16And he came to Nazareth, where he had been brought up: and, as his custom was, he went into the synagogue on the sabbath day, and stood up for to read.

17And there was delivered unto him the book of the prophet Esaias. And when he had opened the book, he found the place where it was written,

[18]The Spirit of the Lord is upon me, because he hath anointed me to preach the gospel to the poor; he hath sent me to heal the brokenhearted, to preach deliverance to the captives, and recovering of sight to the blind, to set at liberty them that are bruised,

[19]To preach the acceptable year of the Lord.

[20]And he closed the book, and he gave it again to the minister, and sat down. And the eyes of all them that were in the synagogue were fastened on him.

[21]And he began to say unto them, This day is this scripture fulfilled in your ears.

Luke 4:16-21

John the Baptist was a man who knew the Scriptures as he himself was a fulfilment of them. John was the voice of the one crying the wilderness, prepare ye the way of the Lord. The miracles, signs and wonders we have seen in the Church to date are nothing compared to what will be seen in the new dispensation of *power* and *glory*. The piercing of this spirit of the Sadducees will usher in that move of God.

What is the sign of the Prophet Jonah?

Jesus responded to the Sadducees and said only the sign of the prophet Jonah would be given to them.

[1]The Pharisees also with the Sadducees came, and tempting desired him that he would shew them a sign from heaven.

[2]He answered and said unto them, When it is evening, ye say, It will be fair weather: for the sky is red.

[3]And in the morning, It will be foul weather to day: for the sky is red and lowering. O ye hypocrites, ye can discern the face of the sky; but can ye not discern the signs of the times?

[4]A wicked and adulterous generation seeketh after a sign; and there shall no sign be given unto it, but the sign of the prophet Jonas. And he left them, and departed.

Matthew 16:1-4

It is thought that Jonah lived in approximately 860 BC. He had been instructed by God to go to a town of *One Hundred and Twenty* thousand people to preach the word of God but he disobeyed.

[1]Now the word of the LORD came unto Jonah the son of Amittai, saying,

[2]Arise, go to Nineveh, that great city, and cry against it; for their wickedness is come up before me.

> *³But Jonah rose up to flee unto Tarshish from the presence of the LORD, and went down to Joppa; and he found a ship going to Tarshish: so he paid the fare thereof, and went down into it, to go with them unto Tarshish from the presence of the LORD.*
>
> *⁴But the LORD sent out a great wind into the sea, and there was a mighty tempest in the sea, so that the ship was like to be broken.*

Jonah 1:1-4

Note that Jesus asked a rhetorical question of the Sadducees, "Can you not discern the signs of the times?" In other words, the sign of Jonah will tell us where in the timing of God we are. The last verse in the book of Jonah describes the situation of Nineveh at the time of Jonah.

> *¹¹And should not I spare Nineveh, that great city, wherein are more than sixscore thousand persons that cannot discern between their right hand and their left hand; and also much cattle?*

Jonah 4:11

It says they could not discern between their right hand and their left hand. This implies a state of confusion and lack of judgement.

Is it possible that the great depression hitting nations of the earth is an indication that believers are escaping from divine instructions?

In these present times, the evidence of confusion is at the highest level it has ever been. It seems that all efforts to stabilise the economic and political boats of nations are not producing the desired results. It is obvious that the so called knowledgeable ones in these matters are resorting to trial and error to determine the best socioeconomic policies to pursue. Nations are falling into deep recession; even churches are collapsing due to an inability to meet financial commitments. One must ask if such churches actually understand the mysteries of the kingdom.

Is the sign of Jonah still speaking today?

Jonah escaped from divine instruction and boarded a ship to escape the presence of the Lord. This action brought a great wind into the sea and there was a mighty tempest so strong, the ship was almost broke apart.

Is it possible that the great depression hitting nations of the earth is an indication that believers are escaping from divine instructions? Is the fact that many believers are finding themselves in the *belly of whales* an indication that divine instructions are being violated? The second chapter of Jonah talks about three days and three nights in the belly of a fish.

> *[17]Now the LORD had prepared a great fish to swallow up Jonah. And Jonah was in the belly of the fish three days and three nights.*

> Jonah 1:17

While we know that this also signifies the death, burial and resurrection of Jesus the anointed One, is it be possible that the great fish that has swallowed up a lot of believers now is the path that will deliver them to the place of predestination?

Finally, the story of Jonah strikes at the very heart of the doctrines of the Sadducees. It presents the message of the resurrection after three days and multiple supernatural occurrences that can only be described as a spiritual interference in the affairs of men. These things represent the very thoughts that the Sadducees denied.

These strange supernatural occurrences in the affairs of men will bring to pass the dispensation of His power and glory. The outcome of which will see nations turning to the Lord for deliverance. Nations of the earth are crying out of God. Is this the situation Paul described in the book of Romans when he wrote about the expectation of creation?

> *[19]For the earnest expectation of the creature waiteth for the manifestation of the sons of God.*

> Romans 8:19

Let us step out in faith, speaking the Word of God boldly and with authority. Creation is crying out for us and expectation is high in the hearts of men. The time for the harvest is here, the Lord is willing and we are ready.

12

The spirit of the Sadducees in the Financial Order

his evil spirit invades the high echelons of ruling councils and organisations particularly financial and political organisations. Churches are not exempt from this invasion. This invasion ensures that policies, laws and other vehicles that facilitate the smooth running and governing of the people are not geared towards liberty but bondage forcing the people to consistently focus on self-preservation.

> [12]*And Jesus went into the temple of God, and cast out all them that sold and bought in the temple, and overthrew the tables of the moneychangers, and the seats of them that sold doves,*
>
> [13]*And said unto them, It is written, My house shall be called the house of prayer; but ye have made it a den of thieves.*
>
> [14]*And the blind and the lame came to him in the temple; and he healed them.*
>
> [15]*And when the chief priests and scribes saw the wonderful things that he did, and the children crying in the temple, and saying, Hosanna to the son of David; they were sore displeased,*

Matthew 21:12-15

Reading this account from Matthew, we know that the presence of the spirit of the Sadducees turned the house of prayer into a den of thieves. Jesus not only took out the order that was instituted by the spirit of the Sadducees, He instantly replaced it with the original intention of God for the temple by healing the blind and the lame there. This is what the next dispensation of God for the Church is about, demonstrating the power and glory of the kingdom of God.

> *If our strategies are the same as those of the kingdoms of this world then there is a spiritual problem that needs to be addressed*

After Jesus did these miracles in the temple, it was the chief priests, the scribes and the sect of the Sadducees who were displeased and offended. Jesus had just abolished forty-six years of tradition (*John 2: 20*) and reinstated the true purpose of the temple.

Jesus commanded the doves to be taken out of the temple and not to make His Father's house a house of merchandise or a den of thieves.

> *[12]After this he went down to Capernaum, he, and his mother, and his brethren, and his disciples: and they continued there not many days.*
>
> *[13]And the Jews' passover was at hand, and Jesus went up to Jerusalem.*
>
> *[14]And found in the temple those that sold oxen and sheep and doves, and the changers of money sitting:*
>
> *[15]And when he had made a scourge of small cords, he drove them all out of the temple, and the sheep, and the oxen; and poured out the changers' money, and overthrew the tables;*
>
> *[16]And said unto them that sold doves, Take these things hence; make not my Father's house an house of merchandise.*
>
> *[17]And his disciples remembered that it was written, The zeal of thine house hath eaten me up.*

John 2:12-17

The words Jesus used were strong words because He understood the gravity of the deception that was taking place in the temple. People who had seen this temple and the activities going on there would have been misled about the true purpose of the temple. The word "thief" according to the gospel of John, refers to the one that comes to steal, kill and destroy. In other words we could say that, based on the activities taking place in temple, the temple had become a place where divine instructions were stolen, spiritual dreams killed and Godly destiny destroyed.

> *[10]The thief cometh not, but for to steal, and to kill, and to destroy: I am come that they might have life, and that they might have it more abundantly.*

John 10:10

Jesus further addressed those that sold doves, knowing what doves symbolised in the temple. In Scripture a dove is usually a symbol for the Holy Spirit, as was evident during the baptism of Jesus. We need to be careful that we are not deceived by godly symbols that mask deeds that are far from the truth. These actions were misleading for people. We justify such actions today as a means of supporting the work of the ministry, but God is able to provide for Himself. With such actions, we risk holding programs with more focus on the money to be made rather than the needs of the people being need to be met. People naturally sow seeds, when their needs are met.

The sale of godly artefacts as a means for temple preservation is not one supported by Jesus. The manifestation of glory is enough to produce temple preservation. In the church today, it seems the sale of godly artefacts has taken on a new dimension. Church commerce is the order of the day. Strange items are being sold in the name of ministry preservation. God has His ways of providing for the needs of the church. If our strategies are the same as those of the kingdoms of this world then there is a spiritual problem that needs to be addressed. A lot of believers trust more in the wisdom they get from ungodly sources when really they should trust in Godly wisdom for the running of their estates.

Significant and prolonged lack may be evidence of us not being in the place of appointment because material blessings are always present in the place of appointment. If our methods and ways are the same as those of the kingdoms of this world then it implies that we may have lost our connection with spiritual instruction. When Jesus sent out His disciples to go and preach, He specifically instructed them not to take anything for the journey. So, how were they supposed to survive?

> *[7]And he called unto him the twelve, and began to send them forth by two and two; and gave them power over unclean spirits;*
>
> *[8]And commanded them that they should take nothing for their journey, save a staff only; no scrip, no bread, no money in their purse:*
>
> *[9]But be shod with sandals; and not put on two coats.*
>
> *[10]And he said unto them, In what place soever ye enter into an house, there abide till ye depart from that place.*

Mark 6:7-10

The instruction Jesus had given was able to make the necessary provision at the appointed time. Remember, when the children of Israel left Egypt and walked in the wilderness for forty years, God fed them with manna from above, their clothes did not grow old and their feet were not swollen even though they walked continually.

If our ability to get creative financial thoughts becomes impotent, our choices are limited.

In these days a lot of ministers are finding it hard to accept speaking engagements if a *financial deposit* has not been made. This effectively cuts out ministry to those who lack cash. God, who justifies the ungodly, has ensured that the anointing in this new dispensation does not rest on the select few. It will become common place for miracles to occur in the streets by the unlearned and uneducated.

It is interesting that most of the time such *financial deposits* are only required when the anointing of God has brought such ministers to prominence. When they struggled for recognition, such thoughts were far off. Is the voice of the Holy Spirit in the deposit paid? God is arising and justifying the meek.

Once, in the ministry of Jesus, His disciples came to Him saying, *"there is one casting out devils in Your name and he is not one of us"*. Jesus' response was phenomenal:

> *[38]And John answered him, saying, Master, we saw one casting out devils in thy name, and he followeth not us: and we forbad him, because he followeth not us.*
>
> *[39]But Jesus said, Forbid him not: for there is no man which shall do a miracle in my name, that can lightly speak evil of me.*
>
> *[40]For he that is not against us is on our part.*

Mark 9:38-40

Jesus said, *"Forbid him not....he that is not against us is on our part"*. The impartation and manifestation of the anointing does not require membership in any committee or organised group. It is the relationship with Jesus that produces the miracles and not the membership in any organised group. This man was not one of the twelve disciples, yet he got similar results. A lot of people that will break free from this spirit of the Sadducees and believe in the name of Jesus will get Godly results like they had been with Him. The anointing is not a respecter of persons, groups, denominations or societies. We are in the time of the scourge of small cords. The glory is being restored in the temple.

Why the financial order?

Finances represent our reward for effort. It is the output of creative and productive thinking. It is the evidence of problems being solved and the currency that causes the realisation of dreams. If our ability to get creative financial thoughts becomes impotent, our choices are limited. We become exposed and vulnerable because our defence is destroyed. Finances determine the degree to which we can answer the questions of life.

> [12]*For wisdom is a defence, and money is a defence: but the excellency of knowledge is, that wisdom giveth life to them that have it.*

Ecclesiastes 7:12

> [19]*A feast is made for laughter, and wine maketh merry: but money answereth all things.*

Ecclesiastes 10:19

While our trust is not in finances but in the Lord, finances represent a necessary weapon for the end time. The lender controls the affairs of the borrower. The borrower will always be a servant to the lender.

> [11]*The rich man's wealth is his strong city, and as an high wall in his own conceit.*

Proverbs 18:11

> [7]*The rich ruleth over the poor, and the borrower is servant to the lender.*

Proverbs 22:7

A significant amount of funding for the economy of the western world is coming from sources and organisations whose core beliefs contradict the founding beliefs of these western economies. This is a sign but the Church will restore dignity as supernatural sources of wealth will once again be discovered by the Church.

A similar kind of source is described when Peter raised an issue with Jesus regarding a tax bill.

> [24]*And when they were come to Capernaum, they that received tribute money came to Peter, and said, Doth not your master pay tribute?*
>
> [25]*He saith, Yes. And when he was come into the house, Jesus prevented him, saying, What thinkest thou, Simon? of whom do the kings of the earth take custom or tribute? of their own children, or of strangers?*
>
> [26]*Peter saith unto him, Of strangers. Jesus saith unto him, Then are the children free.*
>
> [27]*Notwithstanding, lest we should offend them, go thou to the sea, and cast an hook, and take up the fish that first cometh up; and when thou hast opened his mouth, thou shalt find a piece of money: that take, and give unto them for me and thee.*

Matthew 17:24-27

Similar sources will be discovered in these days. Water will flow from rocks again as the Church takes its place again.

Every dream killed is a potential future financial stream aborted.

In *Daniel 10:1-21*, an angel had appeared to Daniel in a vision delivering a message from God. In the vision, the angel talked about the prince of the kingdom of Persia being a hindrance to him until Michael, one of the chief angels of God came to help. It is important to note that this angel remained in this spiritual location with the kings of Persia until he got help. It was only after Michael came to offer assistance that the angel could cross into the realm in which Daniel could receive the message.

> [13]*But the prince of the kingdom of Persia withstood me one and twenty days: but, lo, Michael, one of the chief princes, came to help me; and I remained there with the kings of Persia.*

Daniel 10:13

In *Daniel 11:2*, we are told a little bit more about these four kings of

Persia. One of these four kings is going to be differentiated by riches and these riches represented the medium by which he was going to show his strength.

> [2]*And now will I shew thee the truth. Behold, there shall stand up yet three kings in Persia; and the fourth shall be far richer than they all: and by his strength through his riches he shall stir up all against the realm of Grecia.*

Daniel 11:2

We need to be able to engage the enemy in the area of material substance or we will find ourselves as servants in the day of war. I understand that there may be a physical application of these kings to nations of the earth but the prince of Persia that warred with this angel was not a physical prince. Michael, the angel that helped was not a physical being. The kings talked about here cannot be physical. These kings are spiritual rulers of the darkness of this world that have access to certain spiritual storehouses of riches. These treasures were not meant for the devil. They are meant for man, the original ruler of this domain.

Let us look at some important reasons for this attack on finances:

Finances are a catalyst for dreams

Every dream killed is a potential future financial stream aborted. Finances are a necessary catalyst in the realisation of a dream. Finances do not represent the most important ingredient but it is a required ingredient. This spirit of the Sadducees in operation in ruling councils in the temple suppresses dreams. It causes people to trade prayer, their source of life, for outward appearances of seemingly supernatural wisdom.

Finances are a physical evidence of Sonship.

Wealth only multiples in the hand of the wealthy. Most people think the wealthy have their riches because life has dealt the right cards to them, as though life was a gambling expedition. Most unsuccessful people think successful people are successful by chance. This is not completely true. The idea that made most successful people the success they are is usually stumbled on. However, the practical steps that led to the realisation of the idea in tangible form are deliberate ones.

There is a deep famine or recession in the land and many sons are not coming to their senses

---

Increase in financial strength is the product of right judgement. Our ability to receive a divine instruction or idea from God is by being born again. The practical steps needed for execution comes from tutors and governors.

> *[1]Now I say, That the heir, as long as he is a child, differeth nothing from a servant, though he be lord of all;*
>
> *[2]But is under tutors and governors until the time appointed of the father.*
>
> *[3]Even so we, when we were children, were in bondage under the elements of the world:*
>
> *[4]But when the fulness of the time was come, God sent forth his Son, made of a woman, made under the law,*
>
> *[5]To redeem them that were under the law, that we might receive the adoption of sons.*
>
> *[6]And because ye are sons, God hath sent forth the Spirit of his Son into your hearts, crying, Abba, Father.*
>
> *[7]Wherefore thou art no more a servant, but a son; and if a son, then an heir of God through Christ.*

Galatians 4:1-7

The absence of tutors and governors in the life of a believer indicates waste. Our first natural source of tutelage is our parents. If parenting was something we paid for, what price would we put on it. The impact of such training, especially when they are from Godly parents, cannot be valued. They set our minds on the things of God. Their stories of the manifested hand of God provide seeds of faith that make us profitable.

For example, my father, a clergyman himself, taught me discipline with his life. Though highly educated, his humility is astonishing. He is the greatest physical role model life has given me and I am eternally grateful. My mother on the other hand demonstrated what it means for a woman to submit to her husband. Though accomplished in her own right, her depth of love for God was unquestionable. She always believed in her children no matter what. I am still living under the influence of the prayers offered to God by these two remarkable people. What a privilege to have been born to them.

One thing is clear. It is not the child that determines when true sonship manifests; it is at the time appointed by the Father. The prodigal son asked for his share of his inheritance while his father was still living; he asked before the time appointed by the father:

> [11]*And he said, A certain man had two sons:*
>
> [12]*And the younger of them said to his father, Father, give me the portion of goods that falleth to me. And he divided unto them his living.*
>
> [13]*And not many days after the younger son gathered all together, and took his journey into a far country, and there wasted his substance with riotous living.*
>
> [14]*And when he had spent all, there arose a mighty famine in that land; and he began to be in want.*
>
> **Luke 15:11-14**

He wasted the resources through riotous living caused by the wrong judgement of timing and it was only a famine that brought this erroneous lifestyle to light. This young man came to his senses and returned to his father's house. There is a deep famine or recession in the land and many sons are not coming to their senses. They are justifying themselves and blaming the law makers, and everyone else rather than repenting and returning to the Father. There is no famine in the place or timing of appointment by the Father. There is always a surplus of ideas and visions when operating in the Father's timing. Every substance we have carries within it the seed of reproduction at the right time. There is a time of incubation in the womb and this timing depends on the type of seed and womb carrying the seed. Different beings have different timings. The timing in the womb is determined by the being carrying the seed. We should be careful to ensure that our error of timing does not terminate the delivery of our ideas.

The owner of finances determines the dream that lives

Money does not have a characteristic of itself. It takes on the characteristics of the person in whose hand it finds itself. Money moves impulsively with those who have impulsive tendencies and diminishes with wrong judgement. It increases in the hands of those who add value.

^{12}*He said therefore, A certain nobleman went into a far country to receive for himself a kingdom, and to return.*

^{13}*And he called his ten servants, and delivered them ten pounds, and said unto them, Occupy till I come.*

^{14}*But his citizens hated him, and sent a message after him, saying, We will not have this man to reign over us.*

^{15}*And it came to pass, that when he was returned, having received the kingdom, then he commanded these servants to be called unto him, to whom he had given the money, that he might know how much every man had gained by trading.*

^{16}*Then came the first, saying, Lord, thy pound hath gained ten pounds.*

^{17}*And he said unto him, Well, thou good servant: because thou hast been faithful in a very little, have thou authority over ten cities.*

^{18}*And the second came, saying, Lord, thy pound hath gained five pounds.*

^{19}*And he said likewise to him, Be thou also over five cities.*

^{20}*And another came, saying, Lord, behold, here is thy pound, which I have kept laid up in a napkin:*

^{21}*For I feared thee, because thou art an austere man: thou takest up that thou layedst not down, and reapest that thou didst not sow.*

^{22}*And he saith unto him, Out of thine own mouth will I judge thee, thou wicked servant. Thou knewest that I was an austere man, taking up that I laid not down, and reaping that I did not sow:*

^{23}*Wherefore then gavest not thou my money into the bank, that at my coming I might have required mine own with usury?*

Luke 19:12-23

We should start to believe our heavenly Father to lead us to the place of appointment. Only then can we begin to give life to the Godly dreams that will demonstrate the goodness of God to mankind.

13

The spirit of the Sadducees in the Family

A s I mentioned in the vision I saw, the second understanding that came to me, was regarding the family. I thought about what this meant and the Holy Spirit began to shine His light.

The Last Family

I initially thought this related to individual families, but then I began to see a greater picture as the Holy Spirit brought the concept of the first family and the last family to my attention. The first family represents Adam and Eve while the last family represents Jesus and the Church.

> *14For this cause I bow my knees unto the Father of our Lord Jesus Christ,*
> *15Of whom the whole family in heaven and earth is named,*

Ephesians 3:14-15

Paul did not refer to the family in heaven and the family on earth. That would have implied there were two families, which would have required more than one Father. Paul refers to the family in Heaven (Bridegroom) and Earth (Bride, the Church) with one Father.

I now understand that what this evil spirit did in the first family is exactly what it plans to do in the last; effect a change of lineage for members of the family. However, there is a significant difference between these two families.

> *45And so it is written, The first man Adam was made a living soul; the last Adam was made a quickening spirit.*

1 Corinthians 15:45

Our heavenly Father created the first family in Adam and Eve and planted them in a garden east of Eden. He later *manifested* the last family,

Jesus and the Church in the crucifixion and resurrection of Jesus. Adam and Eve, like most things in the Old Testament, represented a shadow of what God was going to do. God's response to the fall of Adam was not reactive, things happened according to the foreknowledge of God; according to God's original plan.

> *Adam and Eve only represented the shadow created by the spirit of deception blocking the revelation of the true Christ.*

A shadow gives an idea of form, shape or size. It is impossible to determine the substance of a thing from its shadow. Imagine the frustration of somebody trying to explain the organs of your body, the operation of your mind and emotions and the functioning of your spirit man from your shadow. It takes someone who understands the real thing to explain the shadow. It is the Holy Spirit, the One who searches the mind of God that can explain the intent of God to humanity. This Holy Spirit is in the Church and the believer.

A shadow is cast when a non-transparent object stands in the way of light. There are no shadows in God. He is Light and there is no variableness in Him. God does not want to restore us to the position Adam and Eve had in the garden. Adam and Eve only represented the shadow created by the spirit of deception blocking the revelation of the true Christ. Remember, the revelation of Adam we have in scripture was an Adam that had not partaken of the tree of life. This is why the Scripture refers to him as a living soul and not a quickening spirit.

> *[22]And the LORD God said, Behold, the man is become as one of us, to know good and evil: and now, lest he put forth his hand, and take also of the tree of life, and eat, and live for ever:*
>
> *[23]Therefore the LORD God sent him forth from the garden of Eden, to till the ground from whence he was taken.*
>
> *[24]So he drove out the man; and he placed at the east of the garden of Eden Cherubims, and a flaming sword which turned every way, to keep the way of the tree of life.*
>
> **Genesis 3:22-24**

There is no record of Adam giving life to anything. When he left Eden, he left with residual life as the fountain of life had ceased. This is like an employee paid a salary by his employer and able to put some money away in savings. If he loses his source of income, that is, his job, he is able to live on his savings and create the appearance of an income for a while. If this income stream is not restored, he will soon be left empty.

The ability to quicken only comes from Jesus by the Holy Spirit. Using the same example above, the situation for the quickening spirit will be different. The employee is never disconnected from the source of income; if one source stops another one is instantly activated without a loss in flow. The Holy Spirit in us quickens our mortal body so the life of God can flow through us.

> [11]*But if the Spirit of him that raised up Jesus from the dead dwell in you, he that raised up Christ from the dead shall also quicken your mortal bodies by his Spirit that dwelleth in you.*

Romans 8:11

We can only understand true life from the quickening spirit and not the living soul. Christ is the true image of God the Father and not Adam. The complete nature of God is found in Christ and not Adam. The fact that a second Adam is talked about in Christ is evidence that some things could not be achieved with the first Adam.

> [11]*If therefore perfection were by the Levitical priesthood, (for under it the people received the law,) what further need was there that another priest should rise after the order of Melchisedec, and not be called after the order of Aaron?*
>
> [12]*For the priesthood being changed, there is made of necessity a change also of the law.*

Hebrews 7:11-12

Let us look at some differences between these two Adam's.

Christ was tempted yet without sin but Adam sinned

We know that while Jesus took on the same earthly form as Adam, He was tempted like Adam, yet he did not sin. It was necessary for

Adam to have overcome sin to enter into true life but he failed in that endeavour.

⁵Let this mind be in you, which was also in Christ Jesus:

⁶Who, being in the form of God, thought it not robbery to be equal with God:

⁷But made himself of no reputation, and took upon him the form of a servant, and was made in the likeness of men:

⁸And being found in fashion as a man, he humbled himself, and became obedient unto death, even the death of the cross.

⁹Wherefore God also hath highly exalted him, and given him a name which is above every name:

Philippians 2:5-9

¹⁵For we have not an high priest which cannot be touched with the feeling of our infirmities; but was in all points tempted like as we are, yet without sin.

Hebrews 4:15

Though God, Jesus came to the earth in the likeness of man. He suffered in the hands of men to bring life to us. Adam was not sacrificed for anybody and he was not a lamb. Adam brought death into the world through his sin while Christ restored life through death, the greatest sting of the enemy. Jesus made an open show and triumphed publicly over death, signifying that the power of the enemy had been destroyed over the soul and the body.

God was Father to Christ and Lord God to Adam

We have no record of Adam calling God father. In the beginning, God, *Elohim* created Adam in *Genesis 1;26*. It was the Lord God, Jehovah, the redemptive One that formed him in *Genesis 2:7*. It is only this relationship of *Lord God* that Adam had with the Almighty God.

Someone might wonder how this kind of relationship is possible. Let me give you an example. A married man that works for an employer has an employer-employee relationship while at work. This same man has a husband-wife relationship with his wife while at home. The activities in this man's life at any point in time are determined by which relationship is active. The man cannot take the expression of husband-wife intimacy into the employer-employee relationship neither can he enforce employer-employee policy in the husband-wife relationship. At least in his right senses, he should not.

Adam was not part of the creators of the garden nor did he have an audience with God before creation. He was the beneficiary of the creation.

When Jesus came, he boldly declared his oneness with the Father. He is said, "*I and the Father are one*". The father relationship encompasses multiple revelations of the names of the Almighty God and everything about Him is revealed in the name Jesus. The depth of the relationship between Adam and the Lord God are incomparable to the relationship between Christ and the Father.

⁹Wherefore God also hath highly exalted him, and given him a name which is above every name:

¹⁰That at the name of Jesus every knee should bow, of things in heaven, and things in earth, and things under the earth;

¹¹And that every tongue should confess that Jesus Christ is Lord, to the glory of God the Father.

Philippians 2:9-11

When Jesus talked about Himself as the bread of life, and the relationship He had with the Father, many of his disciples could not help but say that, "*this is a hard thing to hear*". The revelation of the true Christ is a hard thing to hear for those that are not chosen.

⁵⁷As the living Father hath sent me, and I live by the Father: so he that eateth me, even he shall live by me.

⁵⁸This is that bread which came down from heaven: not as your fathers did eat manna, and are dead: he that eateth of this bread shall live for ever.

⁵⁹These things said he in the synagogue, as he taught in Capernaum.

⁶⁰Many therefore of his disciples, when they had heard this, said, This is an hard saying; who can hear it?

⁶¹When Jesus knew in himself that his disciples murmured at it, he said unto them, Doth this offend you?

⁶²What and if ye shall see the Son of man ascend up where he was before?

⁶³It is the spirit that quickeneth; the flesh profiteth nothing: the words that I speak unto you, they are spirit, and they are life.

⁶⁴But there are some of you that believe not. For Jesus knew from the beginning who they were that believed not, and who should betray him.

⁶⁵And he said, Therefore said I unto you, that no man can come unto me, except it were given unto him of my Father.

⁶⁶From that time many of his disciples went back, and walked no more with him.

⁶⁷Then said Jesus unto the twelve, Will ye also go away?

⁶⁸Then Simon Peter answered him, Lord, to whom shall we go? thou hast the words of eternal life.

⁶⁹And we believe and are sure that thou art that Christ, the Son of the living God.

John 6:57-69

The nature of our relationship with God is one that makes the world marvel. How can the God of the whole earth choose to live in man and be one with him? The depths of understanding of this revelation will lead to the manifestation of the glorified Church.

Christ was one with God, Adam was a little lower than God

Jesus declared many times in Scripture that He was one with the Father saying, "*He that has seen Me has seen the Father*". David in the Psalms described man as being a little lower than God.

⁴What is man, that thou art mindful of him? and the son of man, that thou visitest him?
⁵For thou hast made him a little lower than the angels, and hast crowned him with glory and honour.

⁶Thou madest him to have dominion over the works of thy hands; thou hast put all things under his feet:

Psalms 8:4-6

God refers to this positioning of Adam in the book of Genesis. Adam was not like God in the knowledge of good and evil and he was not like God in immortality.

This was a state Adam was meant to achieve by eating of the tree of life.

[22]And the LORD God said, BEHOLD, THE MAN IS BECOME AS ONE OF US, to know good and evil: and now, lest he put forth his hand, and take also of the tree of life, and eat, and live for ever:

[23]Therefore the LORD God sent him forth from the garden of Eden, to till the ground from whence he was taken.

[24]So he drove out the man; and he placed at the east of the garden of Eden Cherubims, and a flaming sword which turned every way, to keep the way of the tree of life.

Genesis 3:22-24

The Lord God said that "*man is become as one of us.*" Wasn't Adam already like one of them?

All things were created by Christ, All things were created for Adam

According to the gospel of John, we know that all things were created by Christ, the Word of God. Christ was part of the creative Trinity in the beginning but Adam was not. Christ was part of the "**us**" in *Genesis 3;22*.

[1]In the beginning was the Word, and the Word was with God, and the Word was God.
[2]The same was in the beginning with God.

[3]All things were made by him; and without him was not any thing made that was made.

John 1:1-3

Adam had a garden created and planted for him. Adam was not part of the creators of the garden nor did he have an audience with God before creation. He was the beneficiary of the creation.

[8]And the LORD God planted a garden eastward in Eden; and there he put the man whom he had formed.

Genesis 2:8

All things were made by God and brought to Adam for a name including Eve.

[15]And the LORD God took the man, and put him into the garden of Eden to dress it and to keep it.

Genesis 2:15

Adam was bound by laws, Christ is the Lord of the law

After the creation of Adam, God commanded that he could eat of every tree in the garden with the exception of the tree of the knowledge of good and evil.

[23]And it came to pass, that he went through the corn fields on the sabbath day; and his disciples began, as they went, to pluck the ears of corn.

[24]And the Pharisees said unto him, Behold, why do they on the sabbath day that which is not lawful?

[25]And he said unto them, Have ye never read what David did, when he had need, and was an hungred, he, and they that were with him?

[26]How he went into the house of God in the days of Abiathar the high priest, and did eat the shewbread, which is not lawful to eat but for the priests, and gave also to them which were with him?

[27]And he said unto them, The sabbath was made for man, and not man for the sabbath:
[28]Therefore the Son of man is Lord also of the sabbath.

Mark 2:23-28

Where there is no law, there is no transgression (*Romans 4:15*). God's instruction and its consequence represented a law to Adam. This means the continued relationship Adam was going to have with the Lord God was based on the law that restricted him from accessing the tree of the knowledge of good and evil. The relationship we have with God today is based on faith and not the law and we have this relationship because the grace of God abounds towards us.

[16]Therefore it is of faith, that it might be by grace; to the end the promise might be sure to all the seed; not to that only which is of the law, but to that also which is of the faith of Abraham; who is the father of us all,

Romans 4:16

We have been justified by faith and have peace with God through our Lord Jesus Christ. The law that was put in place that restricted us from accessing life after the fall of Adam has been removed and we can now come boldly before the throne of grace to obtain mercy in our time of need. (*Heb 4:16*)

Our Family Lineage

Throughout scripture, we see great emphasis being placed on lineage, through the listing of numerous genealogies. These scriptures sometimes seem boring to the young believer but God, speaking through them, is saying to us that the understanding of family lineage is important. It helps us understand the inheritance we have in Christ.

In the Old Testament there were nine and a half tribes between which the inheritance was divided. The inheritance was divided according to the instructions the Lord had given Moses and Joshua. One of these tribes included Judah. Christ Himself was of the tribe of Judah and of this tribe, nothing was mentioned concerning priesthood in the Old Testament.

> *[1]And these are the countries which the children of Israel inherited in the land of Canaan, which Eleazar the priest, and Joshua the son of Nun, and the heads of the fathers of the tribes of the children of Israel, distributed for inheritance to them.*
>
> *[2]By lot was their inheritance, as the LORD commanded by the hand of Moses, for the nine tribes, and for the half tribe.*
>
> *[3]For Moses had given the inheritance of two tribes and an half tribe on the other side Jordan: but unto the Levites he gave none inheritance among them.*
>
> *[4]For the children of Joseph were two tribes, Manasseh and Ephraim: therefore they gave no part unto the Levites in the land, save cities to dwell in, with their suburbs for their cattle and for their substance.*
>
> *[5]As the LORD commanded Moses, so the children of Israel did, and they divided the land.*

Joshua 14:1-5

This tracing of lineage interestingly disappears in the New Testament. The books of Matthew and Luke are the only Gospels that show Jesus' genealogy. Matthew's account presents an insightful omission. It traces the genealogy of Christ from Abraham and not Noah, Enoch or Abel. Noah, Enoch and Abel being the three the bible records as faith practitioners prior to Abraham (*Hebrews 11;1-8*). While they exercised faith and by grace they had a relationship with God, there was something about the faith of Abraham that earned him the title of *father of all them that believe* (*Romans 4:11*).

Even Enoch who pleased God and was translated that he should not see death was not given such a title.

Faith is always preceded by a promise. Without a promise there can be no faith.

The depth of Abraham's faith can be attributed to one major fact described in *Romans 4*.

> *[1]What shall we say then that Abraham our father, as pertaining to the flesh, hath found?*
>
> *[2]For if Abraham were justified by works, he hath whereof to glory; but not before God.*
>
> *[3]For what saith the scripture? Abraham believed God, and it was counted unto him for righteousness.*
>
> *[4]Now to him that worketh is the reward not reckoned of grace, but of debt.*
>
> *[5]But to him that worketh not, but believeth on him that justifieth the ungodly, his faith is counted for righteousness.*

Romans 4:1-5

Abraham believed that through faith, it is possible for God to justify the ungodly. This justification manifests in Christ who paid a price at Calvary.

> *[8]But what saith it? The word is nigh thee, even in thy mouth, and in thy heart: that is, the word of faith, which we preach;*
>
> *[9]That if thou shalt confess with thy mouth the Lord Jesus, and shalt believe in thine heart that God hath raised him from the dead, thou shalt be saved.*
>
> *[10]For with the heart man believeth unto righteousness; and with the mouth confession is made unto salvation.*
>
> *[11]For the scripture saith, Whosoever believeth on him shall not be ashamed.*
>
> *[12]For there is no difference between the Jew and the Greek: for the same Lord over all is rich unto all that call upon him.*
>
> *[13]For whosoever shall call upon the name of the Lord shall be saved.*
>
> *[14]How then shall they call on him in whom they have not believed? and how shall they believe in him of whom they have not heard? and how shall they hear without a*

preacher?

[15]And how shall they preach, except they be sent? as it is written, How beautiful are the feet of them that preach the gospel of peace, and bring glad tidings of good things!

[16]But they have not all obeyed the gospel. For Esaias saith, Lord, who hath believed our report?

[17]So then faith cometh by hearing, and hearing by the word of God.

Romans 10:8-17

Abraham believed he could place a demand on God that would touch God's nature, causing God to justify the ungodly based on the declaration of believed words; not based on works. This action of Abraham is the definition of faith. Abraham knew that when he placed a demand on God based on the declaration of words he believed, God would respond by causing the actions required by those spoken words to come to pass. In addition to this, Abraham believed that there was nothing in him that was a hindrance to these actions coming to pass. This kind of action is what the bible refers to as the spirit of faith. (*2 Cor 4:13*)

Faith is always preceded by a promise. Without a promise there can be no faith. This is one reason why a lot of people are frustrated in their faith walk. Faith is action taken based on the inspired promises of God.

[18]Who against hope believed in hope, that he might become the father of many nations, according to that which was spoken, So shall thy seed be.

[19]And being not weak in faith, he considered not his own body now dead, when he was about an hundred years old, neither yet the deadness of Sarah's womb:

[20]He staggered not at the promise of God through unbelief; but was strong in faith, giving glory to God;

[21]And being fully persuaded that, what he had promised, he was able also to perform.

[22]And therefore it was imputed to him for righteousness.

Romans 4:18-22

A lot of believers are missing out on this benefit of the kingdom because even though we live in the dispensation of grace, we are still expecting results by works and not by faith.

> ¹³*We having the same spirit of faith, according as it is written, I believed, and therefore have I spoken; we also believe, and therefore speak;*

2 Corinthians 4:13

Abraham through faith received the blessing of circumcision though he himself was uncircumcised. This is the same way we receive the blessings of the promises of Christ in heavenly places though we are on earth.

> ¹¹*In whom also we have obtained an inheritance, being predestinated according to the purpose of him who worketh all things after the counsel of his own will:*

Ephesians 1:11

> ¹³*For the promise, that he should be the heir of the world, was not to Abraham, or to his seed, through the law, but through the righteousness of faith.*
>
> ¹⁴*For if they which are of the law be heirs, faith is made void, and the promise made of none effect:*

Romans 4:13-14

Let us compare the faith of Abraham to the faith of Noah so we can have a graphic illustration of how faith brings us into a right relationship with God. Both men were faced with a situation in which God was going to destroy a people and God had told them what He was going to do.

> ¹¹*The earth also was corrupt before God, and the earth was filled with violence.*
>
> ¹²*And God looked upon the earth, and, behold, it was corrupt; for all flesh had corrupted his way upon the earth.*
>
> ¹³*And God said unto Noah, The end of all flesh is come before me; for the earth is filled with violence through them; and, behold, I will destroy them with the earth.*
>
> ¹⁴*Make thee an ark of gopher wood; rooms shalt thou make in the ark, and shalt pitch it within and without with pitch.*

Genesis 6:11-14

Following the instruction from God, Noah went and did exactly as he was told. He believed that God was able to bring the floods to destroy the earth as He had said he would. Abraham was in a similar situation to Noah but the expression of his faith gave him a very rare relationship with God. God could not hide anything from Abraham.

> [17]*And the LORD said, Shall I hide from Abraham that thing which I do;*

Looking at *Genesis 18:17-22* carefully, we notice that God never told Abraham what He was going to do with Sodom and Gomorrah; He was in discussion with Abraham about the investigative work that was going to take place concerning the cities but Abraham instantly knew the mind of God.

> [23]*And Abraham drew near, and said, Wilt thou also destroy the righteous with the wicked?*

Genesis 18:23

Abraham, by the spirit of faith, starts to place demands on God based on the nature of God. He was fully persuaded that his faith would cause God to respond to his request to save the cities. Unfortunately, ten righteous people were not found in the cities and God destroyed them. Our faith can cause great things to happen on the earth. We need to start walking in the same spirit of faith so that we can see the hand of God move strongly in our lives.

The intensity of light that is released by this foolishness, the kingdom of darkness cannot withstand.

By this same spirit of faith we become members of the only lineage in the New Testament; the lineage of Christ. We are either for Him or against Him. The whole family of heaven and earth is named through Him. Apostle Peter referred to this generation as a chosen one.

> [9]*But ye are a chosen generation, a royal priesthood, an holy nation, a peculiar people; that ye should shew forth the praises of him who hath called you out of darkness into his marvellous light;*
>
> [10]*Which in time past were not a people, but are now the people of God: which had not obtained mercy, but now have obtained mercy.*

1 Peter 2:9-10

We were not chosen by works, we were chosen by grace through faith.

This concept of lineage is important in our understanding of the spirit of the Sadducees. In scripture, we see John the Baptist identifying the lineage of the Sadducees.

John the Baptist and the Sadducees

In the first encounter of John the Baptist with the Sadducees, he used a strange term to refer to them. "O generation of vipers".

> [7]*But when he saw many of the Pharisees and Sadducees come to his baptism, he said unto them, O generation of vipers, who hath warned you to flee from the wrath to come?*
>
> [8]*Bring forth therefore fruits meet for repentance:*
>
> [9]*And think not to say within yourselves, We have Abraham to our father: for I say unto you, that God is able of these stones to raise up children unto Abraham.*

Matthew 3:7-9

Firstly, the word vipers, comes from a root Greek word meaning *poisonous serpent*. He then used this word in conjunction with *generation* which implies "pro-creation, conception or offspring of a father figure"

Earlier, we expanded the words serpent and *subtil* used in the third chapter of the book of Genesis. Incorporating that expansion here, John's words could have read something like this;

> ***"You offspring of the enchanter that casts a spell in a whisper or hiss that has more ability to come up with crafty counsel to produce ungodly or undesirable results"***

This is important because John, by the help of the Holy Spirit, identified their family lineage. Present in the Sadducees was the same spirit that was in the Garden of Eden.

This same spirit is now rising up in our days. Many people are being deceived today. Crafty counsel is being used to create ways that seem right to natural minds. The place of the Holy Spirit in the believer is being pushed to the background because of the rise of earthly wisdom. Believers are scared of walking in the ways of God because His ways may appear foolish. Oh that we would embrace this *foolishness* that we may do exploits. The kingdom of darkness cannot withstand the intensity of light that is released by this foolishness.

Jesus in the gospel of John confirmed this insight that John the Baptist provided;

[36]If the Son therefore shall make you free, ye shall be free indeed.

[37]I know that ye are Abraham's seed; but ye seek to kill me, because my word hath no place in you.

[38]I speak that which I have seen with my Father: and ye do that which ye have seen with your father.

[39]They answered and said unto him, Abraham is our father. Jesus saith unto them, If ye were Abraham's children, ye would do the works of Abraham.

[40]But now ye seek to kill me, a man that hath told you the truth, which I have heard of God: this did not Abraham.

[41]Ye do the deeds of your father. Then said they to him, We be not born of fornication; we have one Father, even God.

[42]Jesus said unto them, If God were your Father, ye would love me: for I proceeded forth and came from God; neither came I of myself, but he sent me.

[43]Why do ye not understand my speech? even because ye cannot hear my word.

[44]Ye are of your father the devil, and the lusts of your father ye will do. He was a murderer from the beginning, and abode not in the truth, because there is no truth in him. When he speaketh a lie, he speaketh of his own: for he is a liar, and the father of it.

John 8:36-44

He referred to them as being of their *"father"* the devil. This translation of the word "devil" here refers to *"an accuser"*. An accuser needs a broken law to be able to make a case in court. The spirit of the Sadducees always raises accusations that have their foundation in traditions against the family of God. They accused Jesus of many things. On earth, there are only two laws in operation concerning generations; The law of the Spirit of Life in Christ and the law of sin and death.

We cannot descend into earthly wisdom for the generation of heavenly results.

Concerning these laws and traditions, the true gospel of liberty has this
to say;

> *[1]There is therefore now no condemnation to them which are in Christ Jesus, who walk
> not after the flesh, but after the Spirit.*
>
> *[2]For the law of the Spirit of life in Christ Jesus hath made me free from the law of sin
> and death.*

Romans 8:1-2

> *[1]My little children, these things write I unto you, that ye sin not. And if any man sin,
> we have an advocate with the Father, Jesus Christ the righteous:*

1 John 2:1

> *[9]If we confess our sins, he is faithful and just to forgive us our sins, and to cleanse us
> from all unrighteousness.*

1 John 1:9

Anyone who has not given their life to Jesus falls under the lineage of
the devil and anyone who has accepted Jesus as their personal Lord and
Saviour receive the lineage of God and of Jesus.

> *[15]For ye have not received the spirit of bondage again to fear; but ye have received the
> Spirit of adoption, whereby we cry, Abba, Father.*

Romans 8:15

So what changed in the Garden of Eden? It was the lineage of Adam. He
was in the image of God, that is, the form God created for him, until he
obtained inheritance of life and gained immortality. After taking of the
fruit from Eve, their eyes were opened and the lineage changed. They
had received the knowledge of good and evil before partaking in eternal
life.

> *[6]And when the woman saw that the tree was good for food, and that it was pleasant
> to the eyes, and a tree to be desired to make one wise, she took of the fruit thereof, and
> did eat, and gave also unto her husband with her; and he did eat.*
>
> *[7]And the eyes of them both were opened, and they knew that they were naked; and
> they sewed fig leaves together, and made themselves aprons.*

Genesis 3:6-7

We see that the eyes of both of them were not opened until Adam partook of the fruit. Adam was not deceived like Eve. He only loved his wife in his own strength. We have heard it said that the devil deceived Adam and Eve but the bible says otherwise. Had Adam gone to God for wisdom on the restoration of Eve he would have found out that without the shedding of blood, there is no remission of sins.

> *[13]For Adam was first formed, then Eve.*
>
> *[14]And Adam was not deceived, but the woman being deceived was in the transgression.*
>
> **1 Timothy 2:13-14**
>
> *[22]And almost all things are by the law purged with blood; and without shedding of blood is no remission.*
>
> **Hebrews 9:22**

It was the desire of Adam to restore Eve by the partaking of the fruit that shielded them from the true source of Life. Remember, the *Tree of Life* was in the garden; Adam could have eaten of this tree of life to access Godly wisdom for the restoration of Eve. In the family of God, self-preservation is not allowed. It is only total dependence on God that keeps us in the law of the Spirit of Life.

We are in the world but not of the world. We cannot descend into earthly wisdom for the generation of heavenly results. Wisdom from above is always higher than earthly wisdom. This same act of deception that the devil used in the garden is what he is trying to use again; thinking it worked then, it should work now. But glory be to God, the playing field is different.

Firstly, we know that if we are deceived, we have a bridegroom, who is also a high priest, who has sacrificed Himself for His bride. This high priest has sacrificed Himself once, so every time his wife is deceived, the blood that was shed cleanses her and the glory is restored. Our bridegroom has also been tested, but unlike Adam, He did not sin.

[15]For we have not an high priest which cannot be touched with the feeling of our infirmities; but was in all points tempted like as we are, yet without sin.

Hebrews 4:15

His blood does not speak accusation, it speaks justification. Christ died so we may be justified. This justification, is not by the works of our hands; we access this justification by faith. This is to ensure that no one is disadvantaged in life. It does not matter where we were born, what our childhood was like or what experiences we have had in life. Through faith in the finished work of Christ we all have access to the promises of God.

[8]And Cain talked with Abel his brother: and it came to pass, when they were in the field, that Cain rose up against Abel his brother, and slew him.

[9]And the LORD said unto Cain, Where is Abel thy brother? And he said, I know not: Am I my brother's keeper?

[10]And he said, What hast thou done? the voice of thy brother's blood crieth unto me from the ground.

Genesis 4:8-10

[24]And to Jesus the mediator of the new covenant, and to the blood of sprinkling, that speaketh better things than that of Abel.

Hebrews 12:24

The blood of Abel was crying unto God after Cain slew him. Remember that at the time Cain and Abel were born the lineage of Adam had already changed.

The price for this freedom is affordable to every one

Because the blood of the Lamb who was slain from the foundation of the world has been shed, it is impossible for the last family to be destroyed. Every time the accuser lifts his voice against the bride, the testifying of the blood brings deliverance (*Revelation 12:10-11*). This is why the teaching on the blood of Christ is important for the preservation of the family. As long as the blood is present, we will always be the righteousness of God.

> ^{10}*And I heard a loud voice saying in heaven, Now is come salvation, and strength, and the kingdom of our God, and the power of his Christ: for the accuser of our brethren is cast down, which accused them before our God day and night.*
>
> ^{11}*And they overcame him by the blood of the Lamb, and by the word of their testimony; and they loved not their lives unto the death.*

Revelation 12:10-11

We see from the description in *Genesis* that it was the eating of a fruit that changed the lineage, so it is today. It is the eating of the bread of life that restores the lineage.

> ^{47}*Verily, verily, I say unto you, He that believeth on me hath everlasting life.*
>
> ^{48}*I am that bread of life.*
>
> ^{49}*Your fathers did eat manna in the wilderness, and are dead.*
>
> ^{50}*This is the bread which cometh down from heaven, that a man may eat thereof, and not die.*
>
> ^{51}*I am the living bread which came down from heaven: if any man eat of this bread, he shall live for ever: and the bread that I will give is my flesh, which I will give for the life of the world.*

John 6:47-51

Apostle Paul in explaining this new lineage talked about the new creature in Christ. Anyone who has believed and confessed Jesus as the Lord of their lives have access to this new lineage. This new creature is the manifestation of a right relationship with God. Righteousness is not something we have, it is something we are.

> ^{17}*Therefore if any man be in Christ, he is a new creature: old things are passed away; behold, all things are become new.*

2 Corinthians 5:17

> ^{21}*For he hath made him to be sin for us, who knew no sin; that we might be made the righteousness of God in him.*

2 Corinthians 5:21

Knowing this work of the Lamb for His bride, Paul had to say that this state is not achieved by works, but by faith. For most people, it is this simplicity they cannot understand. It is in the foolishness of this process that power is exchanged. This gospel is not hidden. The Holy Spirit guides us into all truth so we may be eternally free.

The price for this freedom is affordable to everyone, no matter their race or the colour of their skin. Christ came that we may have life and have it more abundantly (*John 10:10*)

> *27But God hath chosen the foolish things of the world to confound the wise; and God hath chosen the weak things of the world to confound the things which are mighty;*
>
> *28And base things of the world, and things which are despised, hath God chosen, yea, and things which are not, to bring to nought things that are:*
>
> *29That no flesh should glory in his presence.*
>
> *30But of him are ye in Christ Jesus, who of God is made unto us wisdom, and righteousness, and sanctification, and redemption:*
>
> *31That, according as it is written, He that glorieth, let him glory in the Lord*

1 Corinthians 1:27-31

> *3But if our gospel be hid, it is hid to them that are lost:*
>
> *4In whom the god of this world hath blinded the minds of them which believe not, lest the light of the glorious gospel of Christ, who is the image of God, should shine unto them.*
>
> *5For we preach not ourselves, but Christ Jesus the Lord; and ourselves your servants for Jesus' sake.*
>
> *6For God, who commanded the light to shine out of darkness, hath shined in our hearts, to give the light of the knowledge of the glory of God in the face of Jesus Christ.*

2 Corinthians 4:3-6

Praise God, we only need to accept this by faith to live in its reality. Let us share this reality with others that they may come to the knowledge of our Lord and Saviour.

14

The spirit of the Sadducees in spiritual Warfare

*W*e have established the fact that the spirit of the Sadducees seeks to play down the existence of the spirit realm. This sort of thinking has major impact on faith and spiritual warfare.

> *[8]For the Sadducees say that there is no resurrection, neither angel, nor spirit: but the Pharisees confess both.*

Acts 23:8

Faith, we know, is the evidence of things not seen; the evidence of the existence of the spirit realm.

> *[1]Now faith is the substance of things hoped for, the evidence of things not seen.*
>
> *[2]For by it the elders obtained a good report.*
>
> *[3]Through faith we understand that the worlds were framed by the word of God, so that things which are seen were not made of things which do appear.*

Hebrews 11:1-3

From these verses of scriptures we know that by faith, what we see with our physical eyes was made in the spiritual realm, which we access by our inner man. If this be the case, we can safely conclude that whatever we see with our senses, whether good or bad has its origin in the spirit realm.

By the operation of faith, and the power of the Holy Spirit, a believer can access the spirit realm to draw things into the seen or physical realm; By the same token, an unbeliever, by the operation of a contrary spirit, can access the spirit realm and draw things down.

Nothing enters the physical realm from the spirit realm without being called in.

Nothing enters the physical realm from the spirit realm without being called in. The believer uses the power of the Holy Spirit while the children of perdition use enchantments and divinations.

Let us see an example of this.

> ^{10}And Moses and Aaron went in unto Pharaoh, and they did so as the LORD had commanded: and Aaron cast down his rod before Pharaoh, and before his servants, and it became a serpent.
>
> ^{11}Then Pharaoh also called the wise men and the sorcerers: now the magicians of Egypt, they also did in like manner with their enchantments.
>
> ^{12}For they cast down every man his rod, and they became serpents: but Aaron's rod swallowed up their rods.

Exodus 7:10-12

We see that Moses and Aaron did according to what the Lord had planned but the Egyptian magicians did not waste time in responding with similar works using their enchantments. It was not until the fifth time that the magicians could not replicate what Moses did. This is one of the reasons we do not engage the enemy on just power. We engage on *power* and *glory*. If the *finger of God* is not in a thing, the enemy can replicate it.

> ^{16}And the LORD said unto Moses, Say unto Aaron, Stretch out thy rod, and smite the dust of the land, that it may become lice throughout all the land of Egypt.
>
> ^{17}And they did so; for Aaron stretched out his hand with his rod, and smote the dust of the earth, and it became lice in man, and in beast; all the dust of the land became lice throughout all the land of Egypt.
>
> ^{18}And the magicians did so with their enchantments to bring forth lice, but they could not: so there were lice upon man, and upon beast.
>
> ^{19}Then the magicians said unto Pharaoh, This is the finger of God: and Pharaoh's heart was hardened, and he hearkened not unto them; as the LORD had said.

Exodus 8:16-19

We see another example in the second Chapter of the book of Daniel when the king sought interpretation of his dream.

> ^{1}And in the second year of the reign of Nebuchadnezzar Nebuchadnezzar dreamed dreams, wherewith his spirit was troubled, and his sleep brake from him.

Daniel 2:1

He called the magicians and astrologers of the time to help, but the king had a very unusual request. He wanted interpretation of a dream; a dream he did not make known to the enchanters.

> [5]*The king answered and said to the Chaldeans, The thing is gone from me: if ye will not make known unto me the dream, with the interpretation thereof, ye shall be cut in pieces, and your houses shall be made a dunghill.*

> **Daniel 2:5**

The Chaldeans answered the king in their wisdom and they were wrong. This is the same way rulers of this present time are seeking advice from advisers in whom the Spirit of life does not live.

> [10]*The Chaldeans answered before the king, and said, There is not a man upon the earth that can shew the king's matter: therefore there is no king, lord, nor ruler, that asked such things at any magician, or astrologer, or Chaldean.*

> [11]*And it is a rare thing that the king requireth, and there is none other that can shew it before the king, except the gods, whose dwelling is not with flesh.*

> **Daniel 2:10-11**

See the response that Daniel came back with.

> [16] *Then Daniel went in, and desired of the king that he would give him time, and that he would shew the king the interpretation.*

> [17] *Then Daniel went to his house, and made the thing known to Hananiah, Mishael, and Azariah, his companions:*

> [18] *That they would desire mercies of the God of heaven concerning this secret; that Daniel and his fellows should not perish with the rest of the wise men of Babylon.*

> [19] *Then was the secret revealed unto Daniel in a night vision. Then Daniel blessed the God of heaven.*

> **Daniel 2:16-19**

> [27]*Daniel answered in the presence of the king, and said, The secret which the king hath demanded cannot the wise men, the astrologers, the magicians, the soothsayers, shew unto the king;*

> [28]*But there is a God in heaven that revealeth secrets, and maketh known to the king Nebuchadnezzar what shall be in the latter days. Thy dream, and the visions of thy head upon thy bed, are these;*

> **Daniel 2:27-28**

A similar situation is presenting itself to us in our time. How are we going to respond? Can you see that when Jesus talked about the sign of Jonah he referred to a confusion that will hit the world and only the church will be able to solve?

Apostle Paul also spoke to the Corinthians about this spiritual realm:

³For though we walk in the flesh, we do not war after the flesh:

⁴(For the weapons of our warfare are not carnal, but mighty through God to the pulling down of strong holds;)

⁵Casting down imaginations, and every high thing that exalteth itself against the knowledge of God, and bringing into captivity every thought to the obedience of Christ;

⁶And having in a readiness to revenge all disobedience, when your obedience is fulfilled.

⁷Do ye look on things after the outward appearance? if any man trust to himself that he is Christ's, let him of himself think this again, that, as he is Christ's, even so are we Christ's.

2 Corinthians 10:3-7

Spiritual warfare is real, the weapons are real and the results can be seen in the physical. The weapons of men cannot be used in this warfare. Paul in his letter to the Ephesians talked about the weapons that should be used:

¹⁰Finally, my brethren, be strong in the Lord, and in the power of his might.

¹¹Put on the whole armour of God, that ye may be able to stand against the wiles of the devil.

¹²For we wrestle not against flesh and blood, but against principalities, against powers, against the rulers of the darkness of this world, against spiritual wickedness in high places.

¹³Wherefore take unto you the whole armour of God, that ye may be able to withstand in the evil day, and having done all, to stand.

¹⁴Stand therefore, having your loins girt about with truth, and having on the breastplate of righteousness;

¹⁵And your feet shod with the preparation of the gospel of peace;

¹⁶Above all, taking the shield of faith, wherewith ye shall be able to quench all the fiery darts of the wicked.

¹⁷And take the helmet of salvation, and the sword of the Spirit, which is the word of God:

> [18]*Praying always with all prayer and supplication in the Spirit, and watching thereunto with all perseverance and supplication for all saints;*

Ephesians 6:10-18

If we doubt the existence of this spiritual realm, we do so at our own peril. The principalities, the powers, the rulers of darkness and spiritual wickedness in high places are real.

Warring with Intelligence.

The spirit of the Sadducees is what makes people think it is a battle based on flesh and blood but through our knowledge of the word of God, we persevere in praying, relying totally on the Holy Spirit for spiritual intelligence. Natural armies do not go to war without intelligence. Intelligence makes all the difference in warfare. With the right intelligence, we understand the timing and location of the enemy. This enables us to deploy the right weapons.

> [8]*Then the king of Syria warred against Israel, and took counsel with his servants, saying, In such and such a place shall be my camp.*
>
> [9]*And the man of God sent unto the king of Israel, saying, Beware that thou pass not such a place; for thither the Syrians are come down.*
>
> [10]*And the king of Israel sent to the place which the man of God told him and warned him of, and saved himself there, not once nor twice.*
>
> [11]*Therefore the heart of the king of Syria was sore troubled for this thing; and he called his servants, and said unto them, Will ye not shew me which of us is for the king of Israel?*
>
> [12]*And one of his servants said, None, my lord, O king: but Elisha, the prophet that is in Israel, telleth the king of Israel the words that thou speakest in thy bedchamber.*
>
> [13]*And he said, Go and spy where he is, that I may send and fetch him. And it was told him, saying, Behold, he is in Dothan.*
>
> [14]*Therefore sent he thither horses, and chariots, and a great host: and they came by night, and compassed the city about.*
>
> [15]*And when the servant of the man of God was risen early, and gone forth, behold, an host compassed the city both with horses and chariots. And his servant said unto him, Alas, my master! how shall we do?*
>
> [16]*And he answered, Fear not: for they that be with us are more than they that be with them.*

[17]And Elisha prayed, and said, LORD, I pray thee, open his eyes, that he may see. And the LORD opened the eyes of the young man; and he saw: and, behold, the mountain was full of horses and chariots of fire round about Elisha.

2 Kings 6:8-17

Intelligence provided by the Holy Spirit is always accurate. He never misses a target. Our prayer and supplication should be in the Holy Spirit. We need to be careful of using prescribed methods in spiritual warfare. Jesus warned about using vain repetitions in prayer. It is the intensity and accuracy of praying that makes the difference.

15

Piercing the spirit of the Sadducees

God our Father has made provision for us to be able to overcome this spirit. We have access to wisdom and knowledge through Jesus. While we cannot stop the devil from trying to deceive us, we can certainly choose our response when faced with the issues of life. Let us consider some key facts that will help us overcome the enemy.

The Spirit of Wisdom and Revelation

For the believer, wisdom and revelation are very important. Revelation shows us what to do while wisdom instructs us on how to do it. Without the spirit of wisdom and revelation the mysteries of the kingdom of God will be hidden from us. Paul prayed for the early churches to which he had been sent that God will give them this spirit:

> [15]*Wherefore I also, after I heard of your faith in the Lord Jesus, and love unto all the saints,*
>
> [16]*Cease not to give thanks for you, making mention of you in my prayers;*
>
> [17]*That the God of our Lord Jesus Christ, the Father of glory, may give unto you the spirit of wisdom and revelation in the knowledge of him:*
>
> [18]*The eyes of your understanding being enlightened; that ye may know what is the hope of his calling, and what the riches of the glory of his inheritance in the saints,*
>
> [19]*And what is the exceeding greatness of his power to us-ward who believe, according to the working of his mighty power,*
>
> [20]*Which he wrought in Christ, when he raised him from the dead, and set him at his own right hand in the heavenly places,*
>
> [21]*Far above all principality, and power, and might, and dominion, and every name that is named, not only in this world, but also in that which is to come:*
>
> [22]*And hath put all things under his feet, and gave him to be the head over all things to the church,*
>
> [23]*Which is his body, the fulness of him that filleth all in all*

Ephesians 1:15-23

Jesus also talked about this ability to understand the mysteries of the kingdom of God being given to the followers of Jesus.

> [10]*And the disciples came, and said unto him, Why speakest thou unto them in parables?*
> [11]*He answered and said unto them, Because it is given unto you to know the mysteries of the kingdom of heaven, but to them it is not given.*
>
> **Matthew 13:10-11**

The prophet Isaiah also talked about this spirit of wisdom and understanding resting on Jesus. If Jesus needed this spirit, we certainly need Him. We need to constantly pray that God will increase the measure of this spirit on us like He did with Jesus. The quick understanding we need for this end time, comes as a result of this spirit.

> [2]*And the spirit of the LORD shall rest upon him, the spirit of wisdom and understanding, the spirit of counsel and might, the spirit of knowledge and of the fear of the LORD;*
> [3]*And shall make him of quick understanding in the fear of the LORD: and he shall not judge after the sight of his eyes, neither reprove after the hearing of his ears:*
>
> **Isaiah 11:2-3**

One of the reasons we have the Holy Spirit is to guide us into all truth. It is the truth that makes us free. This is why knowing the Holy Spirit is the greatest asset of a believer in these times. It is the Holy Spirit that brings the "knowing" that Jesus talked about.

> [12]*I have yet many things to say unto you, but ye cannot bear them now.*
> [13]*Howbeit when he, the Spirit of truth, is come, he will guide you into all truth: for he shall not speak of himself; but whatsoever he shall hear, that shall he speak: and he will shew you things to come.*
> [14]*He shall glorify me: for he shall receive of mine, and shall shew it unto you.*
>
> **John 16:12-14**

> [32]*And ye shall know the truth, and the truth shall make you free.*
>
> **John 8.32**

Once the truth of God's word comes to us, we start to get wise in the affairs of life. This is the point at which we start to exchange earthly thoughts for heavenly ones.

¹And I, brethren, when I came to you, came not with excellency of speech or of wisdom, declaring unto you the testimony of God.

²For I determined not to know any thing among you, save Jesus Christ, and him crucified.

³And I was with you in weakness, and in fear, and in much trembling.

⁴And my speech and my preaching was not with enticing words of man's wisdom, but in demonstration of the Spirit and of power:

⁵That your faith should not stand in the wisdom of men, but in the power of God.

⁶Howbeit we speak wisdom among them that are perfect: yet not the wisdom of this world, nor of the princes of this world, that come to nought:

⁷But we speak the wisdom of God in a mystery, even the hidden wisdom, which God ordained before the world unto our glory:

⁸Which none of the princes of this world knew: for had they known it, they would not have crucified the Lord of glory.

⁹But as it is written, Eye hath not seen, nor ear heard, neither have entered into the heart of man, the things which God hath prepared for them that love him.

¹⁰But God hath revealed them unto us by his Spirit: for the Spirit searcheth all things, yea, the deep things of God.

¹¹For what man knoweth the things of a man, save the spirit of man which is in him? even so the things of God knoweth no man, but the Spirit of God.

¹²Now we have received, not the spirit of the world, but the spirit which is of God; that we might know the things that are freely given to us of God.

¹³Which things also we speak, not in the words which man's wisdom teacheth, but which the Holy Ghost teacheth; comparing spiritual things with spiritual.

¹⁴But the natural man receiveth not the things of the Spirit of God: for they are foolishness unto him: neither can he know them, because they are spiritually discerned.

¹⁵But he that is spiritual judgeth all things, yet he himself is judged of no man.

¹⁶For who hath known the mind of the Lord, that he may instruct him? but we have the mind of Christ.

1 Corinthians 2:1-16

This wisdom makes us respond to the instructions of the word of God that has been revealed to us. Revelation is usually followed by instruction. When this instruction is followed, a miracle is birthed. Peter followed an instruction in *Luke 5*, which led to a great multitude of fish. He followed another instruction (*Matt 17:27*), this time, it gave him access to treasures hidden in dark places: the money buried in supernatural store houses. (*Isaiah 45:3*)

> *These hidden things are the thoughts, beliefs and misconceptions about ourselves that we hold.*

Naaman followed an instruction which led to his healing (*2 Kings 5*), the Widow of Zarephath followed an instruction leading to an unending flow (*2 Kings 4*). What instruction are we following?

Renouncing the hidden things of the heart

For us as believers, the most important things are the invisible things of the heart: the things that we do not see. Knowing that our inner man of the heart is the real man that will live forever, we need to make sure that the contents of our hearts are worthy of honour. Jesus said, it is not the things that go into a man that defiles him but what comes out of him (*Matthew 15:18-20*).

We need to renounce hidden things of the heart. It is out of the abundance of the heart that the mouth speaks. The only way to determine the content of a heart is by the words spoken. These hidden things are the thoughts, beliefs and misconceptions about ourselves that we hold. It is the little foxes that destroy destiny. Hurts and offences that are given a place in our hearts block our access to life.

> *[1]Therefore seeing we have this ministry, as we have received mercy, we faint not;*
>
> *[2]But have renounced the hidden things of dishonesty, not walking in craftiness, nor handling the word of God deceitfully; but by manifestation of the truth commending ourselves to every man's conscience in the sight of God.*
>
> *[3]But if our gospel be hid, it is hid to them that are lost:*
>
> *[4]In whom the god of this world hath blinded the minds of them which believe not, lest the light of the glorious gospel of Christ, who is the image of God, should shine unto them.*
>
> *[5]For we preach not ourselves, but Christ Jesus the Lord; and ourselves your servants for Jesus' sake.*
>
> *[6]For God, who commanded the light to shine out of darkness, hath shined in our hearts, to give the light of the knowledge of the glory of God in the face of Jesus Christ.*
>
> **2 Corinthians 4:1-6**

Scripture warns us to guard our heart with all diligence for out of it flow the issues of life. In another place it says out of the abundance of the heart the mouth speaks. We cannot depend on other things in addition to the Word of God.

Passion becomes lust when the object of the passion is not a God given desire.

Our heart is the place where doubt or faith is processed. These hidden things stop the promises of God from flowing into our lives. King David said, *"if I regard iniquity in my heart, the Lord will not hear my voice"*. If we do not walk in faith, we will not get Godly results.

[14] *But every man is tempted, when he is drawn away of his own lust, and enticed.*

James 1:14

The devil cannot create new passions in you that God did not already put there. He can only contaminate existing passions (*lusts*). Passion becomes lust when the object of the passion is not a God given desire.

In dealing with hidden things of the heart, one of the most important things we need to get rid off is called offences.

Offences – a hidden thing of the heart

Offences in the heart need to be gotten rid off. Offences are the accusations we hold against others. These accusations give the enemy the right to bring accusations against us. Offences are a stumbling block in a walk of life. Offences are usually caused by our insufficient understanding of situations. We always want our choices to be the right ones. I once heard someone say *"we judge ourselves by our thoughts while we judge others by their actions."* We wonder why people do not just do what we think; if they did the world would be a better place.

Offences usually take place when the Lord is working. This is usually because He uses the foolish things of this world to confound the wise. When Jesus talked about the leaven of the Pharisees and Sadducees, he immediately warned about offences. This is because offences cut us off from the power of God.

38Now it came to pass, as they went, that he entered into a certain village: and a certain woman named Martha received him into her house.

39And she had a sister called Mary, which also sat at Jesus' feet, and heard his word.

40But Martha was cumbered about much serving, and came to him, and said, Lord, dost thou not care that my sister hath left me to serve alone? bid her therefore that she help me.

41And Jesus answered and said unto her, Martha, Martha, thou art careful and troubled about many things:

42But one thing is needful: and Mary hath chosen that good part, which shall not be taken away from her.

Luke 10:38-42

When offences are in the heart, the only words that can come out are accusative words. These accusative words, though spoken to men are usually directed to God. Martha's offence was not with Mary, it was with Jesus. It is hard to get the person you are accusing to also be a mediator. If we can only concentrate on that needful part, we will not fall into the trap of offences.

Jesus warned about offences many times and in *John 6*, He referred to the devil as the father of accusation. When we hold offences in our hearts, we are giving place to the devil. When God works, sometimes envious people get offended. A lot of people were offended with Jesus because of the things He did. Notice *Luke 7:23*

23And blessed is he, whosoever shall not be offended in me.

Luke 7:23

Jesus immediately pronounced a blessing on those who were not offended in him. Offences will arise because when the dispensation changes, traditions will be broken. Though John the Baptist was a prophet, it is not recorded anywhere that he did any miracles. When certain people who represent elders in the church start to see people that are of unlearned origin, by the standards of men getting results they will attack them by raising standards against them. These standards are based on tradition and not the word of God.

The Study of the Word.

Without in-depth study of the Word of God we will not discover things in it. God inspired men to write it. (*2 Tim 3:16*) Without these writings by men who were inspired of the Holy Spirit, we will not get the revelation of God we desperately need. The Word of God is required for the transformation of the mind. This is the only source through which the mind of a believer can be cleansed.

> *[1]I beseech you therefore, brethren, by the mercies of God, that ye present your bodies a living sacrifice, holy, acceptable unto God, which is your reasonable service.*
>
> *[2]And be not conformed to this world: but be ye transformed by the renewing of your mind, that ye may prove what is that good, and acceptable, and perfect, will of God.*
>
> *[3]For I say, through the grace given unto me, to every man that is among you, not to think of himself more highly than he ought to think; but to think soberly, according as God hath dealt to every man the measure of faith.*

Romans 12:1-3

The mind is where the instruction of God needs to be for them to be fruitful. These instructions are received through the inner man, our spirit man, and passed on as Godly thoughts, laced, with power to our minds.

> *[14]For if I pray in an unknown tongue, my spirit prayeth, but my understanding is unfruitful.*
>
> *[15]What is it then? I will pray with the spirit, and I will pray with the understanding also: I will sing with the spirit, and I will sing with the understanding also.*

1 Corinthians 14:14-15

Paul is saying here that in order for our understanding to be profitable, the godly words we are releasing in the spirit need to get to the mind. The study of the Word brings us into a place of sound doctrine and it is only sound doctrines that allow mysteries to manifest.

> *[14]But continue thou in the things which thou hast learned and hast been assured of, knowing of whom thou hast learned them;*

[15] And that from a child thou hast known the holy scriptures, which are able to make thee wise unto salvation through faith which is in Christ Jesus.

[16] All scripture is given by inspiration of God, and is profitable for doctrine, for reproof, for correction, for instruction in righteousness:

[17] That the man of God may be perfect, thoroughly furnished unto all good works.

[1] I charge thee therefore before God, and the Lord Jesus Christ, who shall judge the quick and the dead at his appearing and his kingdom;

[2] Preach the word; be instant in season, out of season; reprove, rebuke, exhort with all long suffering and doctrine.

[3] For the time will come when they will not endure sound doctrine; but after their own lusts shall they heap to themselves teachers, having itching ears;

[4] And they shall turn away their ears from the truth, and shall be turned unto fables.

2 Timothy 3:14-4:4

If you do not understand the mysteries we have talked about, you will not be able to get results with them. It will be like a man with a toolbox full of tools that he does not know how to use. He is no better off than the man without the tools.

Teaching brings insight which in turn attracts faith which produces action. Many miracles are being delayed because people lack insight.

Without sound doctrine, we can be derailed. The study of the Word is required if God is going to approve of us. You cannot rightly divide the word of truth by reading or hearing. It is done through study. What is study? It is actively seeking answers on a given subject using the Word of God. When we actively seek out answers, the Holy Spirit shows us multiple dimensions of the mind of God on the given subject. It is this study that brings inspiration to us.

[15] Study to shew thyself approved unto God, a workman that needeth not to be ashamed, rightly dividing the word of truth.

[16] But shun profane and vain babblings: for they will increase unto more ungodliness.

[17] And their word will eat as doth a canker: of whom is Hymenaeus and Philetus;

[18] Who concerning the truth have erred, saying that the resurrection is past already; and overthrow the faith of some.

> [19]*Nevertheless the foundation of God standeth sure, having this seal, The Lord knoweth them that are his. And, let every one that nameth the name of Christ depart from iniquity.*

2 Timothy 2:15-19

The presence of unbelief and the absence of supernatural results is an indication of absent or inadequate teaching of the Word of God. The rightly divided Word of God always eradicates unbelief. We saw earlier that as soon as Jesus was faced with a situation involving unbelief, he increased the intensity of the teaching.

Jesus identified some things that restricted the disciples from doing these great works, particularly *unbelief* and *prayer*.

> [14]*And when they were come to the multitude, there came to him a certain man, kneeling down to him, and saying,*
>
> [15]*Lord, have mercy on my son: for he is lunatick, and sore vexed: for ofttimes he falleth into the fire, and oft into the water.*
>
> [16]*And I brought him to thy disciples, and they could not cure him.*
>
> [17]*Then Jesus answered and said, O faithless and perverse generation, how long shall I be with you? how long shall I suffer you? bring him hither to me.*
>
> [18]*And Jesus rebuked the devil; and he departed out of him: and the child was cured from that very hour.*
>
> [19]*Then came the disciples to Jesus apart, and said, Why could not we cast him out?*
>
> [20]*And Jesus said unto them, BECAUSE OF YOUR UNBELIEF: for verily I say unto you, If ye have faith as a grain of mustard seed, ye shall say unto this mountain, Remove hence to yonder place; and it shall remove; and nothing shall be impossible unto you.*
>
> [21]*HOWBEIT THIS KIND GOETH NOT OUT BUT BY PRAYER AND FASTING.*

Matthew 17:14-21

These two things are again at the heart of what the Sadducees rejected. This unbelief restricts the working of the Word of God.

Right Teaching

Right teaching will eliminate the virus of unbelief. Our desire for the sincere *meat* of the Word of God will cause the revelation of the Spirit to come to us. We should leave the place of the first principles and go on to maturity.

> ¹*Therefore leaving the principles of the doctrine of Christ, let us go on unto perfection; not laying again the foundation of repentance from dead works, and of faith toward God,*
>
> ²*Of the doctrine of baptisms, and of laying on of hands, and of resurrection of the dead, and of eternal judgment.*
>
> **Hebrews 6:1-2**

Our first and primary source of right teaching should be the Holy Spirit. He is the One that reveals secrets.

> ²⁰*But ye have an unction from the Holy One, and ye know all things.*
>
> ²¹*I have not written unto you because ye know not the truth, but because ye know it, and that no lie is of the truth.*
>
> ²²*Who is a liar but he that denieth that Jesus is the Christ? He is antichrist, that denieth the Father and the Son.*
>
> ²³*Whosoever denieth the Son, the same hath not the Father: he that acknowledgeth the Son hath the Father also.*
>
> ²⁴*Let that therefore abide in you, which ye have heard from the beginning. If that which ye have heard from the beginning shall remain in you, ye also shall continue in the Son, and in the Father.*
>
> ²⁵*And this is the promise that he hath promised us, even eternal life.*
>
> ²⁶*These things have I written unto you concerning them that seduce you.*
>
> ²⁷*But the anointing which ye have received of him abideth in you, and ye need not that any man teach you: but as the same anointing teacheth you of all things, and is truth, and is no lie, and even as it hath taught you, ye shall abide in him.*
>
> **1 John 2:20-27**

The anointing of the Holy Spirit which is within and upon the believer gives access to the mind of God on any issue. We need to be able to search the word of God ourselves under the guidance of the Spirit of God. No one knows about the things of God like the Holy Spirit because he searches the mind of God. His leading is always accurate. He produces faith by the illumination and enlightenment He brings.

God has also placed gifts (*teachers*) in the church to help us grow into maturity.

> ¹¹*And he gave some, apostles; and some, prophets; and some, evangelists; and some, pastors and teachers;*
>
> ¹²*For the perfecting of the saints, for the work of the ministry, for the edifying of the*

body of Christ:

[13]Till we all come in the unity of the faith, and of the knowledge of the Son of God, unto a perfect man, unto the measure of the stature of the fulness of Christ:

[14]That we henceforth be no more children, tossed to and fro, and carried about with every wind of doctrine, by the sleight of men, and cunning craftiness, whereby they lie in wait to deceive;

[15]But speaking the truth in love, may grow up into him in all things, which is the head, even Christ:

Ephesians 4:11-15

In the book of Acts, we read the story of an Ethiopian eunuch who was reading the Word of God and needed clarification. His desire for clarification touched heaven and God provided angelic assistance to ensure that revelation and understanding came to him:

[26]And the angel of the Lord spake unto Philip, saying, Arise, and go toward the south unto the way that goeth down from Jerusalem unto Gaza, which is desert.

[27]And he arose and went: and, behold, a man of Ethiopia, an eunuch of great authority under Candace queen of the Ethiopians, who had the charge of all her treasure, and had come to Jerusalem for to worship,

[28]Was returning, and sitting in his chariot read Esaias the prophet.

[29]Then the Spirit said unto Philip, Go near, and join thyself to this chariot.

[30]And Philip ran thither to him, and heard him read the prophet Esaias, and said, Understandest thou what thou readest?

[31]And he said, How can I, except some man should guide me? And he desired Philip that he would come up and sit with him.

[32]The place of the scripture which he read was this, He was led as a sheep to the slaughter; and like a lamb dumb before his shearer, so opened he not his mouth:

[33]In his humiliation his judgment was taken away: and who shall declare his generation? for his life is taken from the earth.

[34]And the eunuch answered Philip, and said, I pray thee, of whom speaketh the prophet this? of himself, or of some other man?

[35]Then Philip opened his mouth, and began at the same scripture, and preached unto him Jesus.

[36]And as they went on their way, they came unto a certain water: and the eunuch said, See, here is water; what doth hinder me to be baptized?

[37]And Philip said, If thou believest with all thine heart, thou mayest. And he answered and said, I believe that Jesus Christ is the Son of God.

[38]And he commanded the chariot to stand still: and they went down both into the water, both Philip and the eunuch; and he baptized him.

> [39]And when they were come up out of the water, the Spirit of the Lord caught away Philip, that the eunuch saw him no more: and he went on his way rejoicing.
>
> [40]But Philip was found at Azotus: and passing through he preached in all the cities, till he came to Caesarea.
>
> **Acts 8:26-40**

In verse 30, Philip asks the question, which in modern day language would have sounded like this. *"Do you understand what you are reading?"* The Lord then met his need by making sure someone was available to provide the much needed insight into the scriptures.

Teaching brings insight which in turn attracts faith which produces action. Many miracles are being delayed because people lack insight. A lot of people are like this eunuch but they do not crave further understanding. It is necessary to have a teachable spirit. This allows us to get a perfect understanding of the Word of God. As we grow in the things of God, we get a deeper understanding of His ways.

A lot of believers miss out on the plan of God because they are not listening to what God is saying presently. While God never changes, He has an agenda that is revealed through time. Our actions should be in line with the timing if we want to see that hand of God moving in our life. This agenda of God is unfolded to the Church progressively.

> [24]And a certain Jew named Apollos, born at Alexandria, an eloquent man, and mighty in the scriptures, came to Ephesus.
>
> [25]This man was instructed in the way of the Lord; and being fervent in the spirit, HE SPAKE AND TAUGHT DILIGENTLY THE THINGS OF THE LORD, KNOWING ONLY THE BAPTISM OF JOHN.
>
> [26]And he began to speak boldly in the synagogue: whom when Aquila and Priscilla had heard, they took him unto them, and expounded unto him the way of God more perfectly.
>
> **Acts 18:24-26**

Revelation is Progressive

We know that revelation is progressive because Apollos was given a more perfect understanding of the word of God. Eloquence and intellectual or theological understanding is not the same as revelation. Apollos was eloquent and mighty in scriptures. He was even diligent, yet he lacked a more perfect understanding of the ways of God.

We see Paul also saying the same thing in his letter as seen in the book of Hebrews.

[11]Of whom we have many things to say, and hard to be uttered, seeing ye are dull of hearing.

[12]For when for the time ye ought to be teachers, ye have need that one teach you again which be the first principles of the oracles of God; and are become such as have need of milk, and not of strong meat.

[13]For every one that useth milk is unskilful in the word of righteousness: for he is a babe.

[14]But strong meat belongeth to them that are of full age, even those who by reason of use have their senses exercised to discern both good and evil.

Hebrews 5:11-14

We know that *milk* here refers to the word of God because Peter also admonished the church the same way and Jesus also highlighted this progressive nature to revelation

[2]As newborn babes, desire the sincere milk of the word, that ye may grow thereby:

1 Peter 2:2

[12]I have yet many things to say unto you, but ye cannot bear them now.

[13]Howbeit when he, the Spirit of truth, is come, he will guide you into all truth: for he shall not speak of himself; but whatsoever he shall hear, that shall he speak: and he will shew you things to come.

[14]He shall glorify me: for he shall receive of mine, and shall shew it unto you.

John 16:12-14

There were many things Jesus wanted to say that he could not say because the timing was not right. However, with the Holy Spirit given to the church, we can now access these things. The key to rightly dividing these words is what we see in verse *14*. *He shall glorify me*. If the revelation you get is from the Holy Spirit, it will not contradict any of the words Jesus spoke when he was on earth, or any words we have in the bible.

God has placed people like Phillip, Priscilla and Aquila in the church to help us grow in the understanding of the Word of God. The word of God not rightly divided leads to destruction but the entrance of the word gives light and understanding to the simple.

Praying in the Spirit.

Looking at this story again, Jesus emphasizes the need for prayer in order to get results:

> [14]*And when they were come to the multitude, there came to him a certain man, kneeling down to him, and saying,*
>
> [15]*Lord, have mercy on my son: for he is lunatick, and sore vexed: for ofttimes he falleth into the fire, and oft into the water.*
>
> [16]*And I brought him to thy disciples, and they could not cure him.*
>
> [17]*Then Jesus answered and said, O faithless and perverse generation, how long shall I be with you? how long shall I suffer you? bring him hither to me.*
>
> [18]*And Jesus rebuked the devil; and he departed out of him: and the child was cured from that very hour.*
>
> [19]*Then came the disciples to Jesus apart, and said, Why could not we cast him out?*
>
> [20]*And Jesus said unto them, Because of your unbelief: for verily I say unto you, If ye have faith as a grain of mustard seed, ye shall say unto this mountain, Remove hence to yonder place; and it shall remove; and nothing shall be impossible unto you.*
>
> [21]*Howbeit this kind goeth not out but by prayer and fasting.*
>
> **Matthew 17:14-21**

When we pray in the spirit, that is, in tongues we bypass our human understanding and we speak mysteries to God.

> [2]*For he that speaketh in an unknown tongue speaketh not unto men, but unto God: for no man understandeth him; howbeit in the spirit he speaketh mysteries.*
>
> **1 Corinthians 14:2**

These mysteries lead to the building up of our spirit man. If our inner man is built up and active, floods of Godly thoughts will find their way into our minds and bring true transformation.

> *[4]He that speaketh in an unknown tongue edifieth himself; but he that prophesieth edifieth the church.*

> **1 Corinthians 14:4**

> *[20]But ye, beloved, building up yourselves on your most holy faith, praying in the Holy Ghost,*

> **Jude 1:20**

The Holy Spirit is the one that helps our infirmities in prayer. He is the one that brings the unknown to us. Sometimes we are not clear on the prayer points, but the Holy Spirit is available to help this infirmity.

> *[26]Likewise the Spirit also helpeth our infirmities: for we know not what we should pray for as we ought: but the Spirit itself maketh intercession for us with groanings which cannot be uttered.*

> **Romans 8:26**

Remember God answers prayer. He does not delay answers but responds by giving the mind of the Holy Spirit concerning issues.

> *[11]If a son shall ask bread of any of you that is a father, will he give him a stone? or if he ask a fish, will he for a fish give him a serpent?*

> *[12]Or if he shall ask an egg, will he offer him a scorpion?*

> *[13]If ye then, being evil, know how to give good gifts unto your children: how much more shall your heavenly Father give the Holy Spirit to them that ask him?*

> **Luke 11:11-13**

In this scripture in the gospel of Luke, Jesus highlighted that, if they being evil, kept the principle of like for like i.e. ask for bread, get bread; ask for fish, get fish; ask for egg, get egg, How much more, will God keep the same principle. If we ask for the mind of God on an issue, the Holy Spirit who knows God's mind will guide us into accurate prayer points.

> *[11]For what man knoweth the things of a man, save the spirit of man which is in him? even so the things of God knoweth no man, but the Spirit of God.*

> **1 Corinthians 2:11**

If we have the mind of God concerning our needs, we will always get what we ask for. Apostle James highlighted this: You ask and do not receive because you ask amiss. It was not the process of asking that was wrong; it was the content of what was being asked. Prayer is not meant to be spent on desires that are not God given.

> *³Ye ask, and receive not, because ye ask amiss, that ye may consume it upon your lusts.*
>
> **James 4:3**

Notice that Paul in the epistle to the Romans did not indicate a lack of understanding on *"how"* to pray. He indicated a lack of complete knowledge of *"what"* to pray for. It is the lack of insufficient information on the object of our praying that causes the problem.

> *²⁶Likewise the Spirit also helpeth our infirmities: for we know not what we should pray for as we ought: but the Spirit itself maketh intercession for us with groanings which cannot be uttered.*
>
> **Romans 8:26**

When we pray with the help of the Holy Spirit, we cannot go wrong. We pray the perfect will of God concerning issues.

16

Effects of Godly wisdom by the Holy Spirit.

*W*e have emphasised the need to wait to hear from God before moving. Jesus told his disciples to wait until they were endued with Power from on high before going into the world to preach. We know the effect obeying this wisdom had on them. Let us see a few outcomes we can expect for following the Holy Spirit.

The illumination of the Mind.

One of the results of following the Spirit is the renewing of our minds. We become quick to understand, and this understanding has nothing to do with our background. It is not natural wisdom. At a young age, Jesus was in the temple, sitting with tutors and doctors and this young boy demonstrated understanding beyond his years.

> [46]*And it came to pass, that after three days they found him in the temple, sitting in the midst of the doctors, both hearing them, and asking them questions.*
> [47]*And all that heard him were astonished at his understanding and answers.*
>
> **Luke 2:46-47**

> [54]*And when he was come into his own country, he taught them in their synagogue, insomuch that they were astonished, and said, Whence hath this man this wisdom, and these mighty works?*
>
> **Matthew 13:54**

> [15]*And the Jews marvelled, saying, How knoweth this man letters, having never learned?*
>
> **John 7:15**

It happened with Christ, it was replicated in his disciples and the Sadducees could not contest it. The evidence spoke for itself. The word of God makes us wise. It brings understanding to the simple. We need to humble ourselves to obey these words so we can eat the fruit of obedience.

> [13]*Now when they saw the boldness of Peter and John, and perceived that they were unlearned and ignorant men, they marvelled; and they took knowledge of them, that they had been with Jesus.*
>
> [14]*And beholding the man which was healed standing with them, they could say nothing against it.*

Acts 4:13-14

The apostles demonstrated this wisdom in the affairs of life as a result of having been with Jesus. As the people saw what they had done and how they conducted themselves, it reminded them of Jesus. This same thing should be happening today, the world should see the believer and think of Jesus.

If we truly engage the mysteries of the kingdom, our results will be unexplainable based on natural laws and standards.

Unexplainable results in material things.

A lot of believers are satisfied when they get just enough to get by. We stop at the point where our need is met. However, we know that God is able to do exceeding abundantly above what we "*ask*" or "*think*". The widows that came in contact with Elisha had supernatural experiences they did not expect. If we truly engage the mysteries of the kingdom, our results will be unexplainable based on natural laws and standards.

How would we explain how the Israelites were fed in the Old Testament while in the wilderness or how a raven fed Elijah the prophet. Is it the wealth of David or that of Solomon we want to explore? Or is it the supernatural accomplishments of Nehemiah in the building of the temple we want to consider?

These things are real. See what Jesus demonstrated:

> [1]*After these things Jesus went over the sea of Galilee, which is the sea of Tiberias.*
>
> [2]*And a great multitude followed him, because they saw his miracles which he did on*

them that were diseased.

^{3}And Jesus went up into a mountain, and there he sat with his disciples.

^{4}And the passover, a feast of the Jews, was nigh.

^{5}When Jesus then lifted up his eyes, and saw a great company come unto him, he saith unto Philip, Whence shall we buy bread, that these may eat?

^{6}And this he said to prove him: for he himself knew what he would do.

^{7}Philip answered him, Two hundred pennyworth of bread is not sufficient for them, that every one of them may take a little.

^{8}One of his disciples, Andrew, Simon Peter's brother, saith unto him,

^{9}There is a lad here, which hath five barley loaves, and two small fishes: but what are they among so many?

^{10}And Jesus said, Make the men sit down. Now there was much grass in the place. So the men sat down, in number about five thousand.

^{11}And Jesus took the loaves; and when he had given thanks, he distributed to the disciples, and the disciples to them that were set down; and likewise of the fishes as much as they would.

^{12}When they were filled, he said unto his disciples, Gather up the fragments that remain, that nothing be lost.

^{13}Therefore they gathered them together, and filled twelve baskets with the fragments of the five barley loaves, which remained over and above unto them that had eaten.

^{14}Then those men, when they had seen the miracle that Jesus did, said, This is of a truth that prophet that should come into the world.

John 6:1-14

From this scripture, we see a need arising and Jesus filled with wisdom asked a question, though He already knew the answer. He tested Philip, to see if he had received this wisdom.

Many families, many businesses, many ministries and many organisations have lost out in this exponential capacity to multiply material things because they have ignored the "mystery of the seed". The lack in our lives may be a manifestation of our ignorance or disrespect for supernatural wisdom. May the Lord of the heavens, give us grace to identify "*the lad*" in our environment in Jesus Name. Amen.

In order for us to believe that this was not a mistake, but a deliberate activation of an inward ability, Jesus repeated this miracle by feeding another four thousand people. The need on the outside invoked the ability on the inside. These results were not "spiritual" results. They were results that had physically manifested counterparts. We should not be deceived. Our spiritual blessing in Christ commands a physically manifested equivalent.

Let us see the equivalent of this in the early Church:

> [15] *And in those days Peter stood up in the midst of the disciples, and said, (the number of names together were about an hundred and twenty,)*
>
> Acts 1:15

They started out with one hundred and twenty names and then the supernatural infusion by the Holy Spirit came. The more we follow the leading of the Holy Spirit, the more supernatural results we will get.

> [1] *And when the day of Pentecost was fully come, they were all with one accord in one place.*
>
> [2] *And suddenly there came a sound from heaven as of a rushing mighty wind, and it filled all the house where they were sitting.*
>
> [3] *And there appeared unto them cloven tongues like as of fire, and it sat upon each of them.*
>
> Acts 2:1-3

The results were supernatural, considering that Peter preached only one message.

> [40] *And with many other words did he testify and exhort, saying, Save yourselves from this untoward generation.*
>
> [41] *Then they that gladly received his word were baptized: and the same day there were added unto them about three thousand souls.*
>
> Acts 2:40-41

The second time, a miracle had just occurred through the hands of Peter and John, creating the platform for another message. This time, a lame man walked and five thousand souls were saved.

> [1] *Now Peter and John went up together into the temple at the hour of prayer, being the ninth hour.*
>
> [2] *And a certain man lame from his mother's womb was carried, whom they laid daily at the gate of the temple which is called Beautiful, to ask alms of them that entered into the temple;*

³*Who seeing Peter and John about to go into the temple asked an alms.*

⁴*And Peter, fastening his eyes upon him with John, said, Look on us.*

⁵*And he gave heed unto them, expecting to receive something of them.*

⁶*Then Peter said, Silver and gold have I none; but such as I have give I thee: In the name of Jesus Christ of Nazareth rise up and walk.*

⁷*And he took him by the right hand, and lifted him up: and immediately his feet and ankle bones received strength.*

⁸*And he leaping up stood, and walked, and entered with them into the temple, walking, and leaping, and praising God.*

⁹*And all the people saw him walking and praising God:*

¹⁰*And they knew that it was he which sat for alms at the Beautiful gate of the temple: and they were filled with wonder and amazement at that which had happened unto him.*

¹¹*And as the lame man which was healed held Peter and John, all the people ran together unto them in the porch that is called Solomon's, greatly wondering.*

Acts 3:1-11

¹*And as they spake unto the people, the priests, and the captain of the temple, and the Sadducees, came upon them,*

²*Being grieved that they taught the people, and preached through Jesus the resurrection from the dead.*

³*And they laid hands on them, and put them in hold unto the next day: for it was now eventide.*

⁴*Howbeit many of them which heard the word believed; and the number of the men was about five thousand.*

Acts 4:1-4

Again, the evidence speaks for itself. Notice in verse *1*, it was the Sadducees that rose up. Be not deceived, the manifestation of this same spirit exists in our time, but God has given us the victory for Jesus triumphed over the enemy and made an open show of it. By faith, we will not be a victim of life, but will release words of faith that will create the environment we desire just as God did in the book of Genesis. The same Word and the same Spirit that was at work in the beginning is also at work in us today.

The manifestation of Healing on a large scale.

Healings on a large scale is one of the signs we will see in these days, I remember a great woman of God saying, *the day is coming when every sick person in meetings will be healed.*

The days of this anointing are not coming, they are here.

As in the Old Testament where there was not one feeble amongst them, so it will be in these last days. Strong healing unction's will be present at our meetings. There will be a significant increase in miraculous healings. Missing body parts will be restored. The same way Jesus took the ear of the soldier that was cut off and restored it, people with mutilated bodies will run to the church and be instantly healed because the power of the Lord will be present to heal.

The days of this anointing are not coming, they are here.

> [15]*But so much the more went there a fame abroad of him: and great multitudes came together to hear, and to be healed by him of their infirmities.*
>
> [16]*And he withdrew himself into the wilderness, and prayed.*
>
> [17]*And it came to pass on a certain day, as he was teaching, that there were Pharisees and doctors of the law sitting by, which were come out of every town of Galilee, and Judaea, and Jerusalem: and the power of the Lord was present to heal them.*
>
> **Luke 5:15 –17**

> [12]*And by the hands of the apostles were many signs and wonders wrought among the people; (and they were all with one accord in Solomon's porch.*
>
> [13]*And of the rest durst no man join himself to them: but the people magnified them.*
>
> [14]*And believers were the more added to the Lord, multitudes both of men and women.)*
>
> [15]*Insomuch that they brought forth the sick into the streets, and laid them on beds and couches, that at the least the shadow of Peter passing by might overshadow some of them.*
>
> [16]*There came also a multitude out of the cities round about unto Jerusalem, bringing sick folks, and them which were vexed with unclean spirits: and they were healed every one.*
>
> **Acts 5:12 –16**

Let our expectation for the things of God begin to rise. He is the same yesterday, today and forever. He is the God that does not change. As He provided signs in the early days, He will provide signs in these days.

17

The Revelation of Power and Glory

F inally, there is a change in spiritual timings and I want to leave these thoughts with you. This is the message the Lord put in my heart as I sought to know His ways. I thought over the words wondering whether it was my mind but the level of *"coincidences"* during this season has proven beyond doubt that God is at work.

According to the gospel by Matthew, Jesus warned the disciples about the doctrine of the Pharisees and Sadducees.

[1]The Pharisees also with the Sadducees came, and tempting desired him that he would shew them a sign from heaven.

[2]He answered and said unto them, When it is evening, ye say, It will be fair weather: for the sky is red.

[3]And in the morning, It will be foul weather to day: for the sky is red and lowering. O ye hypocrites, ye can discern the face of the sky; but can ye not discern the signs of the times?

[4]A wicked and adulterous generation seeketh after a sign; and there shall no sign be given unto it, but the sign of the prophet Jonas. And he left them, and departed.

[5]And when his disciples were come to the other side, they had forgotten to take bread.

[6]Then Jesus said unto them, Take heed and beware of the leaven of the Pharisees and of the Sadducees.

[7]And they reasoned among themselves, saying, It is because we have taken no bread.

[8]Which when Jesus perceived, he said unto them, O ye of little faith, why reason ye among yourselves, because ye have brought no bread?

[9]Do ye not yet understand, neither remember the five loaves of the five thousand, and how many baskets ye took up?

[10]Neither the seven loaves of the four thousand, and how many baskets ye took up?

[11]How is it that ye do not understand that I spake it not to you concerning bread, that ye should beware of the leaven of the Pharisees and of the Sadducees?

[12]Then understood they how that he bade them not beware of the leaven of bread, but of the doctrine of the Pharisees and of the Sadducees.

[13]*When Jesus came into the coasts of Caesarea Philippi, he asked his disciples, saying, Whom do men say that I the Son of man am?*

[14]*And they said, Some say that thou art John the Baptist: some, Elias; and others, Jeremias, or one of the prophets.*

[15]*He saith unto them, But whom say ye that I am?*

[16]*And Simon Peter answered and said, Thou art the Christ, the Son of the living God.*

[17]*And Jesus answered and said unto him, Blessed art thou, Simon Barjona: for flesh and blood hath not revealed it unto thee, but my Father which is in heaven.*

[18]*And I say also unto thee, That thou art Peter, and upon this rock I will build my church; and the gates of hell shall not prevail against it.*

[19]*And I will give unto thee the keys of the kingdom of heaven: and whatsoever thou shalt bind on earth shall be bound in heaven: and whatsoever thou shalt loose on earth shall be loosed in heaven.*

[20]*Then charged he his disciples that they should tell no man that he was Jesus the Christ.*

[21]*From that time forth began Jesus to shew unto his disciples, how that he must go unto Jerusalem, and suffer many things of the elders and chief priests and scribes, and be killed, and be raised again the third day.*

[22]*Then Peter took him, and began to rebuke him, saying, Be it far from thee, Lord: this shall not be unto thee.*

[23]*But he turned, and said unto Peter, Get thee behind me, Satan: thou art an offence unto me: for thou savourest not the things that be of God, but those that be of men.*

[24]*Then said Jesus unto his disciples, If any man will come after me, let him deny himself, and take up his cross, and follow me.*

[25]*For whosoever will save his life shall lose it: and whosoever will lose his life for my sake shall find it.*

[26]*For what is a man profited, if he shall gain the whole world, and lose his own soul? or what shall a man give in exchange for his soul?*

[27]*For the Son of man shall come in the glory of his Father with his angels; and then he shall reward every man according to his works.*

[28]*Verily I say unto you, There be some standing here, which shall not taste of death, till they see the Son of man coming in his kingdom.*

Matthew 16:1-28

This account was triggered by the Pharisees and Sadducees asking for a sign. No greater time in the history of the Church has its relevance been questioned. Law after law is being passed to diminish this relevance by removing the thoughts of God from the conscience of society and a gospel of social inclusion is being pushed.

Great persecution is arising for the sake of the gospel of Jesus. Saints are being persecuted at work mentioning of the name of Jesus, for public displays of faith in Jesus and even for responding to the prayer requests of those in need.

The Spirit of the Lord is raising a standard and He is revealing the mind of God in our time by giving us access to the things of the Kingdom of God. The Lord has given me access to this revelation so that the Church will not be in the dark. As Jesus said while He was on earth, He is confirming today. He is pouring out revelation and wisdom that we may confound the spirit of the Sadducees in our time. The overcoming of this spirit will prepare the way for the revelation of the true Christ which will cause the glorified Church to be manifested.

The return of the Lord is sooner than we think. The momentum of activities in the spirit has changed. A new dispensation of *power* and *glory* is here. The Lord has called up the remnant for this time. The *glory* with the *fire* is invading the Church of our Lord Jesus Christ.

This is the sound of the trumpet to awaken those that are sleeping. Awake, for the *glory* of the Lord is here. Decipher the order and let wisdom arise in you.

- He warned about the Leaven of the Pharisees and Sadducees.
- He ensured the revelation of the true Christ.
- He talked about the manifestation of a glorified church.
- He talked about His second coming.

In these last days, as in the beginning, we respond by an outpouring of the Holy Spirit. This outpouring is here. The windows of heaven have opened and all that are willing will obtain grace.

I cannot explain why the Lord will give an unlearned person as me such a revelation, but let the wisdom of it speak for itself. He is more than able to confirm His Word. The Lord has shown me this revelation because the signs of the end-time are closer than we think. When He finished talking to His disciples about this dispensation, He said;

> [28]*Verily I say unto you, There be some standing here, which shall not taste of death, till they see the Son of man coming in his kingdom.*

Matthew 16:28

I do not know how long it will take for this order to be fulfilled, but one thing I do know is that it is not as long as the Church thinks.

We need to start engaging the power of an endless life revealed to us by the Holy Spirit. The hidden beasts of our time are arising but they will not prevail against the glorified Church for they will meet the standard of the true Christ in the glorified Church. They will be confounded by the wisdom of God. The wisdom that the Holy Spirit teaches. The wisdom that is not accessible to natural men. The wisdom that produces results men cannot deny.

The power of the enemy to hold us from this understanding is destroyed now. I declare that the light of the gospel of Jesus penetrates the darkness of mind and thought that has held minds bound. Be enlightened. Be Illuminated in Jesus Name.

Let faith arise in you. Look to Jesus, the author and finisher of our faith, the provider of help and strength in our time of need, our heavenly Priest, the Lamb that was slain from the foundation of the world, the One who is worthy to open the book, the Resurrection and the Life, the first begotten from the dead, the possessor of heaven and earth, who is alive, making intercession for us in the Holy of Holies, in the presence of the Almighty God, the creator of Heaven and earth, the only wise One, the greatest of all, the omnipotent Father, the God who sits in the heavens and makes the earth His footstool, the One whose voice is as the sound of many thunders, the earth shakes at His rising, the angels of His presence cry Holy, Holy, Holy, Lord God Almighty, heaven and the earth are filled with His Glory.

His judgement is true and His wisdom is from everlasting to everlasting. Without beginning of days nor end of years, the Alpha and Omega, the

Beginning and the End, the immortal God, who lives forever and ever. His Word is everlasting from generation to generation, the Author of endless life, the Possessor of eternity, The Father of our Lord Jesus Christ.

To Him be glory and honour forever and ever. Amen.

Prayers for Revelation from the Word of God

The God we serve is a faithful God that never changes. He is the same yesterday, today and forever. If you truly seek to know Him, pray the prayers below until the illumination of the Holy Spirit floods your heart.

[15] For this reason, because I have heard of your faith in the Lord Jesus and your love toward all the saints (the people of God),

[16] I do not cease to give thanks for you, making mention of you in my prayers.

[17] [For I always pray to] the God of our Lord Jesus Christ, the Father of glory, that He may grant you a spirit of wisdom and revelation [of insight into mysteries and secrets] in the [deep and intimate] knowledge of Him,

[18] By having the eyes of your heart flooded with light, so that you can know and understand the hope to which He has called you, and how rich is His glorious inheritance in the saints (His set-apart ones),

[19] And [so that you can know and understand] what is the immeasurable and unlimited and surpassing greatness of His power in and for us who believe, as demonstrated in the working of His mighty strength,

[20] Which He exerted in Christ when He raised Him from the dead and seated Him at His [own] right hand in the heavenly [places],

[21] Far above all rule and authority and power and dominion and every name that is named [above every title that can be conferred], not only in this age and in this world, but also in the age and the world which are to come.

[22] And He has put all things under His feet and has appointed Him the universal and supreme Head of the church [a headship exercised throughout the church],

[23] Which is His body, the fullness of Him Who fills all in all [for in that body lives the full measure of Him Who makes everything complete, and Who fills everything everywhere with Himself].

Ephesians 1:15-23 (Amplified Bible)

[9] For this reason we also, from the day we heard of it, have not ceased to pray and make [special] request for you, [asking] that you may be filled with the full (deep and clear) knowledge of His will in all spiritual wisdom [in comprehensive insight into the ways and purposes of God] and in understanding and discernment of spiritual things--

[10] That you may walk (live and conduct yourselves) in a manner worthy of the Lord, fully pleasing to Him and desiring to please Him in all things, bearing fruit in every good work and steadily growing and increasing in and by the knowledge of God [with fuller, deeper, and clearer insight, acquaintance, and recognition].

^{11} *[We pray] that you may be invigorated and strengthened with all power according to the might of His glory, [to exercise] every kind of endurance and patience (perseverance and forbearance) with joy,*

^{12} *Giving thanks to the Father, Who has qualified and made us fit to share the portion which is the inheritance of the saints (God's holy people) in the Light.*

^{13} *[The Father] has delivered and drawn us to Himself out of the control and the dominion of darkness and has transferred us into the kingdom of the Son of His love,*

^{14} *In Whom we have our redemption through His blood, [which means] the forgiveness of our sins.*

^{15} *[Now] He is the exact likeness of the unseen God [the visible representation of the invisible]; He is the Firstborn of all creation.*

^{16} *For it was in Him that all things were created, in heaven and on earth, things seen and things unseen, whether thrones, dominions, rulers, or authorities; all things were created and exist through Him [by His service, intervention] and in and for Him.*

^{17} *And He Himself existed before all things, and in Him all things consist (cohere, are held together).*

^{18} *He also is the Head of [His] body, the church; seeing He is the Beginning, the Firstborn from among the dead, so that He alone in everything and in every respect might occupy the chief place [stand first and be preeminent].*

^{19} *For it has pleased [the Father] that all the divine fullness (the sum total of the divine perfection, powers, and attributes) should dwell in Him permanently.*

^{20} *And God purposed that through (by the service, the intervention of) Him [the Son] all things should be completely reconciled back to Himself, whether on earth or in heaven, as through Him, [the Father] made peace by means of the blood of His cross.*

Colossians 1:9-20 (Amplified Bible)

^{18} *Open my eyes, that I may behold wondrous things out of Your law.*

Psalm 119:18 (Amplified Bible)

Lightning Source UK Ltd.
Milton Keynes UK
07 October 2009

144654UK00001B/9/P